EURASIA'S NEW FRONTIERS

Eurasia's New Frontiers

Young States, Old Societies, Open Futures

Thomas W. Simons, Jr.

Cornell University Press

Ithaca and London

First published 2008 by Cornell University Press

Printed in the United States of America

Library of Congress Cataloging-in-Publication Data

Simons, Thomas W.
    Eurasia's new frontiers : young states, old societies, open futures / Thomas W. Simons, Jr.
        p. cm.
    Includes bibliographical references and index.
    ISBN 978-0-8014-4743-3 (cloth : alk. paper)
    1. Former Soviet republics—Politics and government.
2. Former Soviet republics—Foreign relations—United
States.   3. United States—Foreign relations—Former
Soviet republics.   I. Title.

    DK293.S58   2008
    947.086—dc22   2008022866

Cloth printing   10 9 8 7 6 5 4 3 2 1

For Peggy

The first time; but then
it always is

"The time has come," the Walrus said,
"To talk of many things:
Of shoes—and ships—and sealing-wax—
Of cabbages—and kings—
And why the sea is boiling hot—
And whether pigs have wings."

LEWIS CARROLL, *The Walrus and the Carpenter*

CONTENTS

Acknowledgments

I was a stranger, and ye took me in.

Matthew 25:35

This little book's path to the light of day began on the Advisory Council of the Kennan Institute for Advanced Russian Studies in Washington, D.C. I joined the council when I retired from the Foreign Service in 1998 for the Stanford history department, and I was serving as council chair in 2001 when my wife and I moved back to Cambridge, Massachusetts, where we had met, after an absence of thirty-eight years. For the first time since I was fifteen, however, I had no position to go to. I was then rescued from terrifying indolence by another Council member, Timothy J. Colton, the director of Harvard's Davis Center for Russian and Eurasian Studies. Tim is a remarkable student of Russian politics whose kindness matches his scholarship, and together with his then associate directors Lisbeth L. Tarlow and Marshall I. Goldman, he and I came up with the idea of a multiyear workshop of academic and government specialists on the

Soviet and post-Soviet space to explore the main trends in its life—the most basic and the most salient—since the fall of Communism in 1991. It was to be called the Program on Eurasia in Transition, I was its director, and I will always be grateful to the Davis Center leadership for making that program possible.

Four times a year from 2002 to 2005, therefore, a core of fifteen to twenty scholars and serving and retired U.S. government officials and a revolving rim of invitees met in Cambridge's Central Square for sessions on trends that are important across the Eurasian landscape: language, say, or religion, or state-building and institutions, or energy, or civil society. Most of our scholars were in mid-career, so their superb expertise was sometimes narrow; the officials had decades of experience in and on the area, but the knowledge it gave them was often inchoate. I knew how to run a meeting. Together, we were able to rise above our prior expertise and experience to more Olympian views—broader, more comprehensive, more synthetic—than each of us had had before. We were not teleological: we had no idea what Eurasia was transitioning to, although we kept the title because we liked the acronym; and the end points sketched out in this book emerged over three years of good work. The views expressed here are very much mine, and I bear sole responsibility for them. But they are enriched by a hundred insights from my colleagues in the program. Many of the scholars among them are cited in the endnotes and the suggestions for further reading, but I salute them all: you know who you are. And I thank you all for the work and the fellowship.

There was then a penultimate phase, before the writing, in the process of crystallization that created this book: my three years as Provost's Visiting Professor at Cornell. Two weeks every February from 2004 to 2006, my wife Peggy and I traveled to upstate New York looking for Siberian winters that never came. Instead, I found warm opportunities in my lectures and seminars to refine the impressions on today's post-Soviet space that had come together in the Harvard program and bring them closer to the region's evolving realities (as I would like to think). For that I am grateful to Professor of Economics and Civil and Environmental Engineering Richard Schuler and his wife, Mary, friends of many years who were most responsible for bringing us to Ithaca; to Provost Carolyn (Biddy) Martin, who spread her hand upon me for my stay; to Professor of International Studies and Government Valerie Bunce, a fellow "Eastologist" whose friendly disagreement often spurred me on; and to the rest of the Cornell community who made us so welcome.

That includes John G. Ackerman, the director of Cornell University Press, and his wonderfully capable staff. "Cast thou they bread upon the waters: for thou shalt find it after many days," says the Preacher (Ecclesiastes 11:1). Their professional skill and personal good will have made the last phase happen and brought this volume to the world. I hope the world will benefit in this time of presidential transition and thereafter; I know I have benefited immensely already.

A final word of gratitude is due to my father and mother, Thomas W. and Mary Jo Simons, the two people who introduced me to the world and then to the wider world in the first place—we sailed for Calcutta for the State Department in 1945, when I was seven—and who made me want to understand and write about it. My father never saw my first book; at ninety-seven, my mother is still going strong enough to riffle through this one.

EURASIA'S NEW FRONTIERS

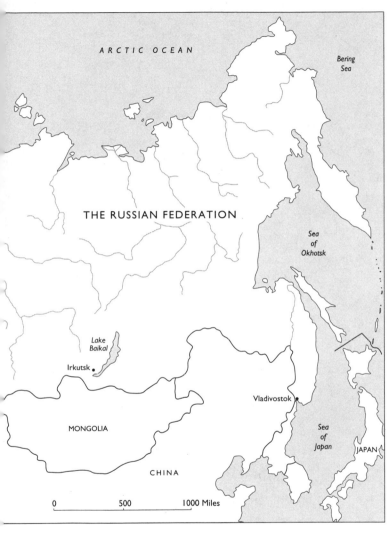

ARCTIC OCEAN

Bering
Sea

THE RUSSIAN FEDERATION

Sea
of
Okhotsk

Lake
Baikal

Irkutsk

Vladivostok

Sea
of
Japan

JAPAN

MONGOLIA

CHINA

0   500   1000 Miles

Eurasia, 2008

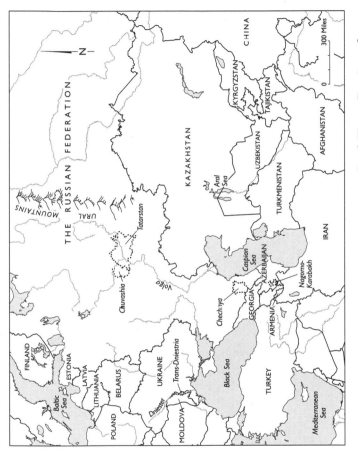

Detail, Western Eurasia, 2008

Introduction: Getting Beyond Eurasia's DNA

"The time has come," the Walrus said . . .

Lewis Carroll

Russia's 2008 presidential election was less suspenseful than ours. Months before the polls on March 2, it was clear that Dmitry Medvedev would succeed Vladimir Putin as president and that Putin would then take over as Medvedev's prime minister. How they work out their cohabitation is an important question for the future, but getting there took political management that would be the envy of any American candidate if it had anything to do with elections. It did not: as the Russian critic and translator Victor Erofeyev lamented in the *New York Times* on election eve, "My vote will make no difference."[1]

All by itself, the distinction between elections like ours, which decide political choices, and elections like Russia's, which merely ratify choices made earlier within the political elite, would signal trouble in U.S.-Russian relations and a problem for U.S. foreign policy. Russia is a big and important country that inevitably engages major U.S. national interests, and we engage better with countries whose values overlap at least partially with ours. A truculent, authoritarian Russia that swings its economic weight in the world for political ends—which is the way more and more Americans see it—is worrisome enough.

But the trouble is in fact larger, for two reasons. First, today's sour Russia was not born yesterday, but has emerged at the end of a decade's descent from something else, all in the post-Soviet era. As Erofeyev put it, "There was a day when it did seem that my vote mattered." He was thinking of 1996, when President Boris Yeltsin came up from single-digit poll ratings to beat his ex-Communist challenger: not so long ago. It is not just that the Russian political scene is cold; it's that it has gotten colder.

Second, it is not just Russia. The same sad trajectory has marked country after country among the new states that used to share the Soviet Union with Russia and that emerged into the same sun of new independence and hope in 1991. Definitions of "Eurasia" can stretch it from Iceland to Alaska, but for the narrower contemporary analytical purposes of this book, it is composed of these fifteen post-Soviet states. To be sure, their trajectories have not been uniform. There is still substantial variety. Despite some inherited pathologies and problems with minority rights, the three Baltic States, now members of the European Union, are very democratic indeed. Earlier in the decade there were "color revolutions" that changed governments in Georgia (Rose), in Ukraine (Orange), and in Kyrgyzstan (Tulip); in February 2008 Armenia joined them as a place where politics from below matters.

And there is more real politics everywhere, even in Russia, than there was in Soviet times. (All are attached to elections, if only because in today's world no country is *hoffähig*—fit to be received at court—without them.) Economic systems show something of the same variety. Yet the general political trend across Eurasia's eleven time zones has been away from democratic hopes toward more authoritarian, more presidential realities. If that is what Americans see when they look at Eurasia, they are not wrong.

What they should do about it is one of the issues that will (or should) be debated in an election year and beyond. Hand-wringing is not good enough for U.S. policy. Nor can Americans fall back on summary explanations that can lead our policy nowhere. Eurasia is too important an area for the United States, and the United States is too important in the world, for shortcuts like that. Such explanations now abound, from history, from culture, from geography, from personality, from "national interests." But for the most part they do not help us understand Eurasia, and therefore leave us helpless when we seek remedies for the problems the region causes us, and when we seek opportunities hidden in the weeds. For it is profoundly true that things happen for reasons, that they have causes, in Eurasia as everywhere else; and there as elsewhere their causes are usually proximate, rooted in the same realities we live in. We can therefore grasp them; but unless we do we will remain mired in mere distaste, drawn to wrong policies toward Russia and its neighbors, or to none at all.

In this book I explore some of those proximate causes

for the political settling or "sedimentation" that has marked Eurasia over the past fifteen or so years, and suggest some realistic approaches for generating effective U.S. policy.

Let me start by summing up the basic argument, and let me do so in operational order, the sequence in which each reality I see determines the next.

First, civil society is anemic across the post-Soviet space. Groups of people engaged in self-chosen activities are there; civil society exists. But it is emerging only slowly from state tutelage. Over the longer term, privatization of the economy and increasing wealth may well create middle classes capable of acting independently of the state in the society and politics of some countries. Middle classes may even emerge sooner in those countries where wealth is based on more than raw materials under state control, since such countries have more incentive to reform. These trends are certainly worth supporting. But in the medium term it will be state policy rather than civil society that determines the shape and direction of national development in Eurasia. To count on civil society to do so over the next few years is a counsel of despair. If not a road to hell, it is surely a road to bitter disillusionment.

Second, in the absence of vigorous civil societies politics in Eurasia is and will continue to be primarily a struggle among elite factions. To some extent that is true everywhere, but it is emphatically true in this part of the world. Factions are differently composed in different places: "clans" predominate in Central Asia, "oligarchs" in Russia and Ukraine. But all are more or less intermingled with the state. It is also true that the political arena is now partly public; that media and political parties serve as vehicles for disseminating facts and views in circles broader than elite factions; that mobilized masses and voters have more scope and importance than before. Almost every post-Soviet country has elections of some kind, and these elections can serve as tests and indicators of power positions. But because power depends fundamentally on patronage networks and access to resources for maintaining them, what is critical to political dynamics across Eurasia are elite views of the leader's staying power. Once the leader's grip on power slips or appears threatened, elites begin to hedge and plot, to position themselves to be on the winning side of change; and across the area such shifting is what triggers political change.

Third, if politics in Eurasia is a struggle of elite factions, those factions mainly struggle about economic resources and sovereignty. One might think that nothing is more concrete than economic resources, and for primordial clans and mafias that may be true. But it turns out that definitions of economic need are as much a function of consciousness as definitions of sovereignty are. Economic situations are as "imagined" as political communities are, and imagined or feared deprivation can drive demands for sovereignty just as urgently. So in the post-Soviet space economic and political goals play off each other both at the base—in a Russian region like Tatarstan—and internationally, because in Eurasia a country's international status depends to an extraordinary degree on access to energy, both for those countries that have it and for those that do not.

I will be looking in on how the interplay of economics and politics has worked out across Eurasia. Russia and Turkmenistan have been central players from the beginning thanks to their exportable fossil fuels, and Kazakhstan and Azerbaijan are joining them as their new oil production comes online. Because producers need markets, interdependencies are multiple, among Eurasian countries themselves and with the outside world.

In the early years after 1991 there was a tendency to separate politics and economics in the name of modernization (and investment). Since Westerners believe such separation is a good thing, we encouraged and applauded it in Eurasia too. Unfortunately, these were also years of economic decline and diminishing welfare for most people. The result across Eurasia was to link market reform to state weakness in the public mind. Since this is a part of the world where everything—civil society, elite factions, and politics, as well as sovereignty—typically depends on the state, across the region the market has been tarnished and tarred as a political goal, while the strong state shines brighter every day.

Where the state is weak or underinstitutionalized, as in Tajikistan or Kyrgyzstan or Russia's North Caucasus, or even Ukraine, restoring (or creating) it is a desired goal, just further away. In states where it looks closer, politics is often geared to it. Restoring or fashioning a strong state is therefore politically appealing to elites throughout the area, and market reform tends to be a casualty: the tentative theoretical and practical fire wall between politics and economics that arose in the 1990s very often collapses. Using its energy resources, resurgent Russia is now more aggressive toward its neighbors than it was then or than it has to be; its neighbors reciprocate with suspicion or paranoia that may or may not be warranted by actual Russian deeds or intentions. Today's Eurasia is not the Soviet Union, but it is coming to resemble the old Soviet Union again in several ways, and one involves this politicization of economics. By trying to abolish politics, by trying to enforce their claim that the only "issues" for public policy were economic and social, the Soviets ensured that *every* issue would be political. By its actions vis-à-vis its neighbors over the past two years, Russia has similarly convinced the world that everything Russians do in the world has political intent, most often malign.

However, Russia's bullying and the corresponding truculence among its neighbors are not a recipe for permanent or intermittent turmoil, precisely because in Eurasia it is the state rather than civil society that is the key variable in politics. Russia is strong compared with all its neighbors, because of its size, its energy resources, and now its recovering self-consciousness and self-confidence. But Russia's neighbors too are filling out and building up their state structures and learning how to use them, in self-defense but not only in self-defense: they too can be nasty to other neighbors. In the normal prospect, pressure and resistance by the new Eurasian states could balance each other out in perpetuity, with real change coming only slowly through accumulations of adjustments at the margin. If such balancing lasts long enough Eurasia could turn into a subsystem of states that the rest of the world would consider normal.

We are not there yet: we should be prepared for the abnormal in Eurasia, and tensions could rise. Even if they do, however, they are unlikely to erupt in the volcanic explosions that punctuated the European twentieth century next door.

Those explosions were fueled by modern nationalism in all its rich variety. Sometimes it was "civic," providing for national identity by choice; more often national identity was ethnoreligious or ethnocultural, inherited (it claimed) rather than chosen. Russia's neighbors in Eurasia are probably more likely than Russia itself to develop into nation-states filled and driven by nationalisms of the latter kind, ethnic and exclusive rather than civic and inclusive.

Here too the reasons are multiple. The other new states are weaker and more desperate than Russia, their sovereignty is more novel and more precious to them, and historically, ethnic-based nationalism has been the classic ideological content for new, vulnerable national states in Eastern Europe, just to the west of them. Many post-Soviet states are already war zones; even when the conflicts with neighbors are frozen, they still generate ethnic hatred. The more vulnerable smaller states are also more likely to reach out to the outside world for help in defending themselves, to bring in the outside world to counterbalance Russia (or, say, Uzbekistan), as the Balkan States reached out to the great powers before 1914. The results are not always bad: using the European prospect has kept the post-Communist leadership afloat in tiny, impoverished Moldova despite its breakaway province of Trans-Dniestria and Russian trade embargoes. It is also true that by courting NATO at long distance, Georgia's post-2003 nationalist rulers have not brought all the country's ethnic enclaves back into the national fold, nor avoided surging domestic opposition in 2007. The nation-state filled up by ethnic nationalism may now be part of Europe's past, but it could still be very much part of Eurasia's future.

Still, there is a hedge: on the evidence so far, post-Communist Russia's own experience and current realities militate against Russia's becoming a nation-state driven by European-style ethnocultural nationalism. With twenty-five million Russians living outside Russia's borders and fourteen to twenty million Muslims within them, the Russian state cannot afford to adopt an ethnic definition of citizenship even if its neighbors can. Here the Soviet tradition of ethnically defined "nationality" also helps, since it was personal and transportable, basically independent of territory. So too is Russian nationalism today. It asserts Russia's status in the world, but it is status almost without ethnic or cultural content. It represents no intrinsic values or superiorities that need to be imposed on others: it seeks only the dignity of the Russian state, free from dictation by others. *Noli mi tangere*—the "Don't Touch Me" or "Don't Tread on Me" of our revolutionary battle flags—is its whole banner. This means that Russia's "claims and visions"[2] for itself, its sense of national identity, will be defined by reputation, by prestige, by Russia's own conduct and by the outside world's reactions to it. It means that the outside world has the power to determine the shape of Russia's futures, even if the challenges are initiated and defined in the first instance by the leaders of the consolidating post-Communist Russian state.

Eccala Eurasia: What does it mean for the U.S. and U.S. policy? I will argue that U.S. policy has been fairly successful in pursuing our national interests in relations with post-Communist Eurasia on the basis of its evolving realities, but that we have paid a price in diffuse goals and dispersed efforts. So I will also argue that given today's tougher, tenser Eurasia, U.S. policy probably cannot remain even fairly successful unless it narrows its agenda and prioritizes its partnerships more stringently.

As befits a great power partial to the political status quo in the world, the U.S. has had a policy toward Eurasia which tracks developments there with lags, as it tries to adjust its value-based goals to emerging new realities, because it can afford such delays. Americans believed in the goals of the original so-called triple revolution it wished to support after 1991—market reform, democratic development, and good neighborliness—so U.S. policy continued to promote them long after market reform had slowed, after regimes had congealed into presidentialism, and while intrastate conflicts bubbled on or simply froze with the connivance of area neighbors, after 1993. After 2003, as Putin's Russia started to renationalize its economy's commanding heights, bully its neighbors, reassert control of civil society, and quash political opposition, the U.S. long remained attached to the "strategic partnership" announced in 2002. This had an upside: most non-Russians simply could not believe Russia's claims that it was simply reacting to a U.S. plot or campaign to keep it from its rightful place in the sun. The downside was that U.S. policy adjusted to the post-2003 Eurasian realities so slowly and in such dispersed order that it was left open to charges of "softness" which were then rebutted by periodic outbreaks of "toughness": vis-à-vis Russia, with other Eurasian states, and in the larger world. Together with the kinds of policy lunges characteristic of dying administrations, such as missile defense in Eastern Europe or independence for Kosova, these in turn fueled Russian dyspepsia. On the surface, the result has been tit-for-tat muscularity massaged and softened by the need to cooperate on vital issues and by a desire on both sides to keep a relationship going. Beneath the surface, each country has been able to sustain a mixed policy of cooperation and confrontation. On our side, the Russia-policy bumper sticker, as a workhorse policy official in the State Department put it in May 2007, has been "cooperate wherever we can, push back whenever we have to."[3] On both sides, policies have been supple enough to adjust to new developments and robust enough to stay alive in the hope of better days under new administrations.

In principle, the U.S. can sustain such a mixed policy forever, but I doubt that it can do so in practice unless we can refine our policy agenda *and* its instrumentalities. We can no longer expect major short-term shifts toward market reform or democratic development in Eurasia, nor can we disengage: we have too many vital interests in play. Moreover, as state after national state consolidates itself, they will be more prone than before to bump up against each other, the weaker among them will be more prone than ever to seek support and sustenance from outside the area, including the U.S., and we will be faced with a series of agonizing choices we do not need.

But some of Eurasia's features that I have identified here are actually saving variables. Just because Putin's Russia is the Eurasian state *least* likely to fill up with eth-nonationalist content, just because its ideology has no "values" to drive it or to export, just because it is almost entirely concerned with the independence and prestige of the Russian state in the world, the world has more lever-age on Russian policy than it ever had on Soviet policy. The outside world can shape Russian policy for the better (by the world's lights) precisely because the resurgent Russian state cares so exclusively about how it is treated by the world.

If we are to help make it happen, however, U.S. policy in Eurasia will need to shift its focus to today's states, to make state-to-state relations its centerpiece. We need not—we cannot—sacrifice core American values: any U.S. policy that does so fails. But in Eurasia we can real-istically promote those values for the long term only by working primarily with states in the short term. For in this part of the world it is only in a context of stable de-velopment of state institutions that civil society and democracy, now so heavily embedded in state structures, can emerge and grow. It may not happen, but that is the only way it *can* happen. To work effectively with Eurasia's states, however, the United States needs to treat them as responsible and capable participants in an international society living by twenty-first-century standards. But that also means we too must act like a responsible twenty-first-century state: a change for the better that we can easily afford to make.

That will be my argument. Even if it is not entirely persuasive, it will at least get us beyond some of the simpler explanations on offer for why Eurasia is currently so grim. In October 2007, for instance, President Bush used one in a good cause. Defending our relationship with Russia against attacks from his right, he also mused that "to reprogram the kind of basic Russian DNA, which is a centralized authority, that's hard to do."[4] He may have been joking a bit, as President Reagan once was joking when he was caught giving the order to bomb Moscow in five minutes by a microphone he thought was dead. President Bush's joke (if that is what it was) was the more unfortunate of the two, however. He was on mike, and the implication that we are dealing with some kind of knout in the Russian gene pool closes down too many U.S. policy options. After all, DNA cannot be changed, and if Russia's is bad the only options are to take the perp to court or let him run wild. If we find similarly bad DNA elsewhere in Eurasia, it only multiplies the problem: cop and perp are too few roles with which to enact serious policy in today's world. That way lies hopelessness, which is unworthy not just of U.S. national interests but of reality. We *can* do better. Things can change in Eurasia, and we can help. If my argument does persuade, we will understand better not just what has been lost over the past fifteen years but what has been created and retained, and what remains possible for the future. *Sursum corda:* lift up your hearts.

I

THE WEAKNESS OF CIVIL SOCIETY

"To talk of many things . . . "
LEWIS CARROLL

Civil society is hard to define but easy to idealize.

Whether we realized it or not, many of us in the West grew up permeated with ideas that set "society" over against state power. They are centuries old. In America, our founders looked to the English philosopher John Locke's defense of the Glorious Revolution of 1688 for legitimation of their resistance to arbitrary royal rule here. Half a century later the Frenchman Alexis de Tocqueville taught us that vigorous voluntary activities independent of the state are the necessary foundation of a healthy democracy. Tocqueville in turn was reaching back to Baron de Montesquieu's eighteenth-century vision of English governance, in which the "intermediate bodies" in society tempered and guided the monarch above and the people below. Tocqueville was seeking a hedge against the new tyrannies spawned by the French Revolution— against Robespierre and Napoléon. He had a French agenda, in other words. But he admired so much about our young republic that we thought he was writing just for us.

In our century the Cold War then locked in the concept that "society" both creates government and must be defended against government. One reason we indicted Soviet Stalinist rule, after all, was that it atomized society—that it left the individual naked and helpless against those in power. As the Cold War drew on, furthermore, it produced first the Soviet dissidents, beginning in the 1960s, and then the civil society that burgeoned in parts of the European East in the 1980s. Civil society thereby took concrete form before our eyes. It was not simply a concept we could share, it was a living instrument of political struggle against Communist dictatorship that we could applaud and encourage. Václav Havel and Charter 77 speaking truth to power; Adam Michnik and Solidarity acting "as if" they were free: these were real people. Their roots might be strange to us: their movements were also revivals of older indigenous political traditions, of intellectuals claiming a "government of souls," traditions that were unlike anything in our politics. But they admired us too, so their local European agendas mattered as little to us as Tocqueville's had.

Then in 1989 these movements triumphed, or so it seemed, all across East Central Europe. Their astonishing success is still fresh in memory after nearly twenty years, and it has made "civil society" a universal positive category in Western political discourse ever since. It is not simply the persistent East European vogue for political parties with *civic* or *citizens'* in their names: free Czechoslovakia began with the Civic Forum; the lead party in Poland's ruling coalition in 2008 was the Civic Platform; even repressed Belarus now has its embattled United Civic Party. The concept's resonance is something larger: whatever the nuances, 1989 made it seem that the very ages—History, as the Marxists used to say—validated civil society as a power in its own right, facing a threatening or at least malign state.

Most historical examples of that kind of civil society have in actual fact come from the West rather than Europe's East, but even on its home ground, civil society has been idealized. More than a reality, it has been a category of thought. In early modern Western Europe, the state emerged first as a distinctive institution, before what we now call civil society. Indeed the state often had a hand in *creating* civil society, as princes reached down to commoners for support against nobilities. One reason the tactic was attractive was that emerging capitalism was freeing some economic activity from state control, so that commoners were gaining resources that were useful to kings. Kings and commoners were nevertheless uneasy allies. States only slowly tolerated the emergence of what we would recognize as a citizenry: groups of politically self-conscious people who recognized each other and were able to work together for common purposes across and beyond kinship and class lines.

As early modern turned to modern in the eighteenth and nineteenth centuries, technology and economics created larger and larger economic units, and the population also organized itself more—into work collectives, into associations, eventually into political parties. Political parties are not the same as civil society, but they are related to it, since they too require some autonomy and some scope for self-chosen activity. Even as new formations came into being, however, subjects and citizens in Western Europe still looked to the state to provide them with resources, to counterbalance other powers, to protect them from the uncertainties of enhanced size and mobility.

In our time, finally, the Information-Technology Revolution—IT-driven globalization—has reshaped units, accelerated mobility, and given a whole new potency to the Image, as distinguished from the Thing. This new revolution has created a series of new dilemmas we still barely understand. The results are not necessarily optimal for citizenship, for classic civil society. As Theda Skocpol has pointed out, in recent decades the mass base of nongovernmental organizations in the U.S. has tended to shrink, so that such organizations typically turn more and more into lobbying outfits staffed by elites and interacting primarily with other elites.[1] Tocqueville saw such free associations as the infantry of our democracy; in our time they are coming more and more to consist only of officers.

If that is the case in old, mature democracies like ours, what should we expect further east, in the societies and states of Central and Eastern Europe and the former Soviet Union? If civil society has been idealized and is under stress in its Western heartlands, should we not expect it to be even less robust and even more tentative and fragile in the post-Communist European East, and especially in the post-Soviet space? We should; and it is.

Civil society was not of course entirely missing from

the history of these regions before it emerged onto the political scene in the 1980s. The old patrimonial states that historically ruled the area—Romanov, Habsburg, and Ottoman empires, Caucasian kingdoms, Central Asian khanates—had after all in some sense arisen from society before "society" existed as a concept. Either they arose from among elites or they had created elites to serve them. In either case they had to struggle to separate themselves from these elites to become or remain autocracies. In early modern Russia the estate system that the tsarist state created to serve it included strong vertical linkages between the tsar and the noble and then the serf in his village. At its base was the family, society's strongest institution here as elsewhere, recognized in law. Around it clustered communal property that protected the family even if in law the land "belonged" to the tsar, and later to nobles. Religious institutions also existed and had legal and social status, even when they were firmly under monarchical control. That went for Muslims too; from the time of Catherine the Great onward, Russia's Muslims lived under a unique system that followed the empire's conquering armies, an apparatus staffed and administered by Muslim scholars applying Islamic law, vetted by tsarist officials who tried to do the same when appealed to.[2] Abolished and then resurrected by the Soviets in 1943, this system has survived them across Central Asia and the Caucasus to this day. Some ingredients of civil society were always there.

Yet it is also true that in Eurasia those makings were fewer and smaller than in the West. Where they existed they were less autonomous, less separate from and more dependent on the state. Economic development and market mechanisms were much more likely to be initiated and controlled by the state east of the Elbe or Oder, rivers that ran north and south through Germany. So were the social groups these states created and that made the states work. To be sure, the tsarist and Communist heritages were not the same. Groups of people engaging in self-chosen activities had more scope under the tsars, unless (until toward the end) those activities were deemed "political."

In what would become the post-Soviet space, seventy years of Communist rule then had the dual effect of both expanding these potential constituent elements of civil society and constraining them still further. Structurally, the state-led forced modernization that began in the late 1920s—Stalinist industrialization, urbanization, collectivization—certainly "socialized" the whole population. It threw groups and individuals together in new conglomerates; it brought them together in new structures that were under the thumb of the state but formally separate from it. That was true even of the ruling Communist Party of the Soviet Union (CPSU), nineteen million strong at the end, not counting family members. Legally the CPSU and the Soviet state remained distinct; in practice they were inextricably intermingled.

In fact, the Party did aspire to total control of all significant activity in both state and society, and this gave it a persistent urge to grind down and subordinate the old civic structures—family and religious institutions—and to create new ones—factories, collective farms, and trade unions. All these were endowed with extensive social functions, but without autonomy. They were the famous "transmission belts" of Stalinism and the early Cold War. The urge to permeate and control might be pursued intermittently, or with greater and lesser intensity. Stalin loosened up on religion during the Great Patriotic War; peasant garden plots multiplied for a while on the collective farms. But the urge to dominate was always there and it always resurfaced. It was part of life for the Soviet Union's peoples for more than seventy years.

Although these institutions were created and controlled by the Party-state, in some sense they really existed, to paraphrase the "really existing socialism" of the Brezhnev era, of the 1970s. They could help define a person's identity as well as a person's social and political position. They were vehicles for real bargaining in society and with the authorities. But most of all they monopolized the Soviet Union's resources, political and economic, to an extent that left very little room for anything resembling independent citizenship. Negotiation went up and down, rather than side to side. Soviet institutions created vertical chains of dependents rather than horizontal networks of protocitizens. They were poor vehicles or incubators for any civil society recognizable as such in classic Western terms.

Less obviously, the same was true of the "nation." Historically the nation has been the West's great integrating institution, above the family and the ethnic group that then emerged above the family over historical time. It is less well known that the nation was also the Soviet Union's most astounding creation during its relatively brief history. "Nationhood," the "groupness" that goes into it, the "nation" that it produces: in West and East alike these notions have all been very much a function of consciousness, of identity, and of institutions, and most especially of the state. Sometimes a nation preceded the national state, as in Poland and Hungary. Sometimes empires created nations that then sought nation-states of their own, as in old Austria-Hungary. Sometimes the nation was the creation of an anational or even antinational state, as in the Soviet case. By the end of tsardom nations-in-consciousness were rampant and proliferating in Eurasia, struggling to grow and create their own states. When tsardom fell, the empire's western fringes struggled loose into the new nation-states of Poland and the Baltic republics, or, in the case of what is now Moldova, into an older but enlarged Romania. When the Bolsheviks took over the rest after 1917 they were therefore hyperconscious of nationalism's challenge to their universal revolutionary mission. They wrestled seriously with nationalism throughout their tenure. It can be argued that in the end it was the nation that did them in. What is harder to argue is that it is the nation that has replaced them.

For the nations the Bolsheviks created starting in the 1920s were of a peculiar sort compared with the examples farther west with which we are more familiar. In general the new Soviet nations were mega-examples of all the other social and civic organizations with which they shared the Soviet space. They owed their origin to what the Harvard historian Terry Martin has baptized the "affirmative action empire."[3] They were created by the Soviet Party-state, and when the Baltic republics and today's

Moldova were reconquered and pulverized at the end of World War II, they were crushed into this same "nation" mold. But these nations were created in order to be controlled. And in this the Soviet Party-state succeeded almost until the end. Indeed, the argument is now made that the end came mainly because it succeeded too well: that beginning in the 1960s the policy of assimilating non-Russian peoples into a new Russian-speaking "Soviet" culture was actually working to the point where their newly created elites took fright, and that this produced the spasm of nationalism that stretched the regime to and then past its limit under Mikhail Gorbachev. In the Baltic republics this involved reconnection to older nationalist traditions; elsewhere nationalism often shone like the new minting it was.[4] By that reading, nationalism and the state structures into which it was growing were troublesome to the Soviets throughout and lethal in the end, but they did not constitute a legacy. They pulled the Soviet Humpty Dumpty from his wall, and no one would put him up again, but they were not—or are not yet—in a position to succeed him. (Once again, the Baltics are the exception; here nationalism's broad societal base rather quickly paved the way to Europe, even if some flagstones—such as secure rights for Russian minorities—have had to be put in place along the way. They will appear less often in the coming chapters.)

This weakness of nationalism outside the Baltics helps explain the curious reversal of the early post-Soviet years: when the CPSU disappeared and the Soviet state disintegrated into fifteen new sovereignties (in terms of international recognition), the nations they had created in their seventy years of rule were not yet capable of replacing the Soviet state with nation-states on the Western model or of filling the hearts and minds that the CPSU and its ideology had vacated. In the post-Soviet space, the nation was not—or is not yet—a mega–civil society face-to-face with the powers that had been or the powers that now came into being.

In the early years after the dissolution of 1991, the consequence was a lot of debility without much renewal. But it was hard to tell at the time. In those years the weakness of nationalism was masked by a number of simulacra of broad and deep nationalisms that sprang up in various places. In the first half decade or so there was a good deal of mass mobilization across the old Union's eleven time zones. Workers struck, often for back pay. Demonstrations unrolled against Moscow, against regional and local bosses, against injustice, against alien rule, or just for maintenance of services. The ideologies that drove them could be nationalist or ethnic or, more rarely, imperial. Mass passions could turn military, as in the civil wars that broke out all along the Soviet Union's fringes: in the South Caucasus in Nagorno-Karabakh between Armenia and Azerbaijan and three regions with non-Georgian populations in Georgia; to the West, in Moldova's Russian-speaking Trans-Dniestria; in Tajikistan in Central Asia, where four regions plunged into civil war. Even where wars were averted there were huge tensions: in the Baltic republics, in Ukraine, across Russia. In Russia's Chechnya, war indeed broke out in 1994, abated in 1996, and broke out again in 1999. These were years of streets full of people. Next door in post-Communist Poland, strikes and demonstrations were perhaps a safety valve for discontent at the rigors of market reform under "shock therapy."[5] Even in the post-Soviet space it is possible to theorize differences between a "movement" society and a civil society so as to carve out a future for the latter.[6] For very many people in Eurasia, however, the seemingly endless turmoil of those first years generated a specter of chaos, and perhaps bloody chaos. After all, even closer to Europe, ex-Yugoslavia showed the way.

A good deal of Western policy and Western aid directed toward this new world region in these early years focused on structures that would channel mobilized passions into new economic, political, and social structures that could stabilize over time. But it is worth remembering that at the outset the main emphasis was not on civil society but on the economy. Most Western aid efforts were led and funded by governments, and since governments are most comfortable dealing with other governments, that was where most of the aid went. Paradoxically, its top priority was to help these new governments shrink themselves: at the top of the agenda were macroeconomic policies that would take economies out of the state hands that had held them tight for so many decades and that would permit political and social energies to develop and flourish freely. The next priority was humanitarian: to keep people alive as fraying state social security nets and economic ties were adjusted to market conditions. What technical assistance there was also went mainly to economic institutionalization. Reform and institutional development in politics and society, including civil society, took a distant third place. It was only as humanitarian crises abated and economies settled into their new hybrid shapes that assistance programs turned more to politics and society. It was only then, in the mid-1990s, that "building civil society" became an aid target sector of choice. And by then the local state had begun to reassert the preeminence that is traditional for states in this part of the world.

The featured mechanism to assist civil society has been aid to develop nongovernmental organizations (NGOs). Usually it takes the form of technical advice with some modest funding. Helping NGOs has meant helping some of the area's most attractive people, people who are brave, idealistic, and often Western oriented. It is also fairly cheap, and that too has been attractive as the post-Soviet world becomes less astonishing and political support for aid slips. Finally, aid to NGOs has usually been easier to manage and document, because it is less susceptible to fraud and corruption than economic aid to governments or entrepreneurs. It is not so politically charged—sexy but also dangerous—as assistance to political organizations, say for election monitoring, party formation, efficient parliaments, or issue promotion, or as assistance in building the rule of law, say by training judges and prosecutors.[7] But NGO support has a family resemblance to such aid, under the rubric of building civil society, and they have often been bundled together in budgets. Among those who supported and implemented NGO assistance, there were often high hopes of "roll-out" and "forward linkages" that would bring large returns for small investments in terms of "growing" civil society.[8]

Such hopes were not altogether implausible. In the ruins of the Soviet Union's collapse many new things were possible, and many more *seemed* possible. As an example, the environmental movement had had its small beginnings earlier: it was under the Party general secretary Yuri Andropov in the early 1980s that environmental protection was accepted as a goal of Soviet state policy for the first time, and among the early successes of late Soviet civil society was the effort to save Lake Baikal. But the movement gained enormous momentum in the 1990s. With the state's social safety net tattering everywhere, local self-help efforts in the health field were born and took on vigorous new life. Important areas of the economy were privatizing. As the state receded, new private economic initiative was needed and required, and individuals and autonomous groups had at least potential access to new resources to conduct it.[9] Political power was also decentralizing in very many areas of the post-Soviet space, including Russia. This gave new scope not only to separatism, to ethnic and religious passion and nationalism, but also to constructive or benign civic action.

There was change for the better. How much and how far depended a great deal on the country and the locality, and the actual forms and contents were often mixed. What looked like a new civil society might well turn out to be the creation and creature of local power structures. At a national level parties and youth organizations like Nashi ("Ours") in Russia could suddenly appear in vociferous support of the powers that be.[10] Sponsors in a country's capital might well inspire and support civic organizations in a region in order to undermine or control its local boss. Yet such organizations could also take root independently, particularly when they were based, say, on family-run charitable foundations. Some of the most hardy had no ties at all with the West.

Especially over the first years, therefore, there was very substantial expansion of the range of initiatives from below, not instigated by the state and not under the total control of the state. This was of course a feature of the economy as segments of it privatized. Already by mid-decade the internal grain trade in Russia had basically escaped central direction, even though grain production remained collectivized. But new autonomous activity also marked the media; it marked welfare in an astonishing variety of sectors; and it marked political parties and groups. There were differences in mentality, scale, success, and indeed autonomy; but overall the expansion of civil society was impressive.

Yet after a very few years it started to become apparent to practitioners and researchers alike just how weak the impulse nevertheless was. The causes adduced were multiple; some were not easy to discern given the yawning needs and the din of self-promotion and self-congratulation. Everywhere resources were small, and they got smaller as country after country descended into economic recession.

Even in the most liberalizing economies the state retained a large role, and in those countries where it was largest, as in Central Asia or Belarus, it was simply hard to muster the resources for sustained civic autonomous activity. In Central Asia would-be organizers of civic organizations had to go to the state for offices, for telephones, for cars. So it was in Central Asia that the new phenomenon of the GONGO—the government-organized nongovernmental organization—flourished best.[11] Where the state had receded most from the economy, as in Russia, the wealth it left behind was usually not widely distributed; instead, it was concentrated in relatively few hands, and hence seldom available to support new broad-based civic organizations. If Central Asia and Azerbaijan had their GONGOs, Russia and Ukraine had their "oligarchs." They too could support civic organizations, but the effect was to limit civic autonomy. Where sponsorship was neither central nor private, it was likely to be from regional power coalitions. In many regions of Russia the oligarch was also the political boss. And at the extreme of the "all that glitters" category, when a notorious criminal figure was gunned down outside Yerevan in 2006, the report noted that he had "served since 2000 as the head of [an NGO] advocating the protection of children's rights.[12]

It was no wonder, then, that as the decade of the 1990s drew on, more and more poll respondents answered "family and close friends" when asked whom they looked to for support.[13] Nor was it surprising that the trend paralleled that of answers to the question of whom they "trusted" in political life.

This shrinking and fading of the incipient civil society became more and more apparent with each passing year. Civic organizations had diminishing numbers. Those who remained in the thinning ranks tended to be donor driven; their activities focused more and more on gaining grants and maintaining their foreign support. Without outside funding they turned out to have very little staying power. As utopian hopes faded and despair and fear settled into quotidian mediocrity, NGO dependence on the West provoked more and more nationalist resentment, especially where state relations with the West were souring, as they often were by mid-decade in the new millennium. At that point foreign-supported NGOs became the targets of reconsolidated state power in country after country—Uzbekistan, Belarus, Russia, even Kazakhstan. Sometimes they were able to deflect or soften blows, as in the case of new Russian Federation legislation on NGO registration post-2005, when much of the world community joined the outcry. Generally, though, NGOs have proved powerless to resist. Even under the amended legislation, two years later activist Russian NGOs were "choking on bureaucracy," as a fine report by Human Rights Watch put it.[14] The local states have stepped in to replace the departed foreign funders, naturally at a political price. As one example, the "presidential grants" that Russia's Public Chamber doled out in 2007 to some 1,225 NGOs amounted to $51 million, but the largest went to Putin's youthful acolytes in Nashi.[15] The NGOs that have survived best are usually tied to a family or to the state or both. It is a part of the world where it is still hard to live, much less prosper, without either.

In early 2006 there was a vigorous lobbying campaign against a new pipeline set to skirt Lake Baikal, a project that had been approved by a series of government bodies. The campaign joined outsiders and insiders, but it was capped in April by a vice president of the Russian Academy of Sciences, that is, a dignitary well embedded in the power structure. He addressed President Putin directly.

In response, Putin simply ordered that the route pass at least forty kilometers from the lake; and in May the Irkutsk authorities approved a new route, four hundred kilometers clear of it. It was a victory, and in a good cause.[16] But it vividly recalled Tsar Nicholas I's famous straight railroad line between Moscow and St. Petersburg in the early nineteenth century: where it briefly curved was where his thumb had held the ruler. Progress in both cases, but in both progress by executive fiat.

The blame game started early and has been vigorous ever since. Actual or aspiring Western partners of NGOs in the post-Soviet space have reacted to their emerging or continuing weakness with confusion and even bitterness. A whole scholarly cottage industry has arisen on the derelictions of Western official assistance.[17] The specifics of the bill of indictment may vary—poor administration, inadequate levels, bad targeting, tardiness—but the overall implication is that civil society could have been very much stronger and healthier if only Western governments had done things differently. Sometimes the area partners themselves are blamed: they took too easily to donor dependence, to grant writing, to their nice offices. Usually it is not a matter of individual weakness; sometimes organization is the problem. But culture and history are also called in, in a post-Soviet version of Soviet-era analyses of Russian love of authority, or even colonial-era analyses of Central Asian or Muslim collectivisms. What has been hard to admit is that across the post-Soviet space in the 1990s, there were few foundations for and few available trajectories conducive to flourishing civil societies.

Denial carries with it a danger of overreaction. Faced with the weakness of civil society in so many places, scholars and other analysts are tempted to overlook real if modest achievements, or to redefine civil society in terms of the kinship, clan, and family networks that certainly exist but lack the potential of larger, suprakinship social groupings to affect politics and political systems. As noted earlier, in some localities family charitable foundations may be all the civil society there is. But simply to label kinship-based networks "civil society" distorts the object of study, which is the potential for modernization in society and politics.

Such networks may or may not be the building blocks of the civil societies of the future; but they are not yet the thing itself. And if we equate kinship groups with civil society, we set our expectations for change so low that we overlook real possibilities for further development. As wealth increases and as privatization proceeds in individual sectors, governments across the post-Soviet space will be looking at what might be called Petrine or Chinese development models. For centuries top-down reformers like Peter the Great have dreamed they could import technology and boost economic growth without undesirable political consequences. They want all the benefits of investment and technological innovation without new threats to their power. Today's top-down reformers are no different.[18] They may or may not succeed. But the historical record suggests that top-down development produces new tensions and contradictions that require new political solutions, and that in some polities those solutions in turn require participation by the new groups that top-down reform produces. Civil society's day may be yet to come.

If it is, it is likely to come from within the state in which its ingredients are now entangled. Here conceptual clarity is important. The Tocquevillian or Havelian models pitting civil society against the state may not help illuminate the post-Soviet space or its potential, because these models may not be appropriate to its realities. In February 2006 the former Putin economic adviser Andrei Illarionov excoriated Putin's pulverization of the distinctions between public and private, between politics and economics, in the *New York Times*. Clear-eyed about the staying power of the corporate state arising on the ruins, to fight it Illarionov nevertheless prescribed a Havelian or a Michnikian solution, brewed in the late Communist era: "One can start one's own separation from such a state through a campaign of non-participation. In this way, working from below, one can begin to restore civil, political and economic freedoms."[19] Perhaps; but the advice is desperate. In the post-Soviet space, salvation cannot come only from below.

Civil society is too anemic for that, and it is anemic across the post-Soviet space. Participation rates in organizations are among the lowest in the world, lower even than in post-Communist Central and Eastern Europe; and the data probably understate how low those rates actually are. A hangover from the Soviet experience of compulsory membership in front organizations may help explain why people pitch in so seldom. But after more than fifteen years that explanation is not adequate.

Beginning in 2003, after all, the consolidation of authority across the area was punctuated by the famous series of "color revolutions"—Rose in Georgia in 2003, Orange in Ukraine in 2004, Tulip in Kyrgyzstan in 2005. Once again thousands and hundreds of thousands of people took to the streets for prolonged periods, with tents and toilets and wireless communication. Moreover, Georgian activists had been to Serbia, where peaceful demonstrations had overthrown Slobodan Milošević in 2000; Ukrainian activists had been to Georgia; Kyrgyz activists had been to Ukraine. This was a chain reaction that made governments see democratic development as subversion.[20] But it was also evidence of at least embryonic civil society at work. What form the impulse will take, and how long it will last, are of course questions for the future, but the impulse is there today.

The succession of color revolutions indeed boosted morale and hope among people seeking or waiting for change—for a while. But three years after the last of the series, in Kyrgyzstan, the residues of those hopes are extremely varied. Those three color revolutions had a common origin in electoral fraud, as the next chapter will show, and electoral fraud also loomed large in the new turbulence that again struck Georgia and then Armenia in 2007–8.[21] In all four countries leaders felt they could not prolong their hold on power without it, and that provoked upheaval. But these color revolutions have not had common destinations. Georgia erupted again in late 2007 because the victor in the Rose Revolution was trying to live without an opposition.[22] Ukraine is still mobilized, and its politics are still democratic, but it is moving forward only slowly because every election produces new gridlock. Kyrgyzstan too stays mobilized, but the result is a kind of Brownian motion of demonstrations, negotiations, constitutional changes and elections that manages to leave the balance of forces among the regions that make up the country practically unchanged.

Elsewhere, the impact of the color revolutions has also varied. Together they have made leaders everywhere fear that if they democratize they too will face destabilization by the same methods. Yet leaders have differed in their responses. In some countries there has been crackdown; in others an ooze-and-flow process of tentative, controlled, very carefully paced reform and retrogression; in others careful opening has followed crackdown.

Turkmenistan has illustrated the slow dawn that can follow night. Under the "Father of the Turkmen," Saparmurat Niyazov, the whole country was one big crackdown. Since Niyazov's death, in December 2006, his successor Gurbanguly Berdymukhammedov has steered the country toward something lighter by steps so mild and varied that their rationale is impossible to discern. It is like interpreting the sounds of furniture being moved at the other end of a warehouse. But the language is right: the goals include democratization ("gradual"), strengthening law and order, market reform, and bringing national legislation into line with international law; all are steps that could open up space for civil society.[23]

On a less macro scale, once they have tamed the exuberant quasi–civil society of the early 1990s and the color revolutions and have built some self-confidence, other Eurasian governments are generally willing to grant civil society not just money but some honor—and therefore some political space—as junior partners in the business of governance. Indeed, all Eurasian governments keep a weather eye on their international good reputations, which these days require some tolerance for the human rights and fundamental freedoms that let civil societies function. It probably helps to want something that the international community can give in return. For instance, Chairmanship of the Organization for Security and Co-operation in Europe (OSCE) has been a major objective for Kazakhstan's government, and that may help explain its extraordinary celebration of its own NGOs and civil society, at the very same time its president was tightening his control of elite politics, including his own family. The outside world matters.[24]

It may be no surprise that next door in Kyrgyzstan NGOs have more scope than in most other Eurasian states; Kyrgyzstan has a hard time repressing anything.[25] But even mighty Russia, which can and does repress a lot, has been careful to keep and honor a place for civil society, properly controlled. Scholarly assessments continue to roll in, and to discover—once night has fallen—that Russian NGOs are most successful in achieving their aims when they cooperate with, rather than oppose, the state. Russia also reacts as badly to criticism about NGOs as it does to other criticism.[26] But in the rolling thunder of negative American commentary on Putin's Russia it is still possible to find testimony to the immense fact that while some elite groups may be afraid again, most Russians are not, and not just because many are now connected to the outside world through the Internet and thus no longer isolated.[27] There is still space for Russian civil society to grow.

Ideologically as well, the Putin/Medvedev Russian state has remained pure as the driven snow, and perhaps Medvedev more than Putin. He sounded so different from Putin in his first "campaign" speech that he could not just have been lip-synching: he told thirteen hundred representatives of public organizations that civil society "is an [indisputable] element of political life," pledged that the government "will maintain a steady course toward the development of a free society," and averred that the focus of social policy must be the individual.[28]

The Western Reserve scholar Kelly McMann has brought little Kyrgyzstan and big Russia together analytically, and discovered—again, after night has fallen—that in this part of the world activist individuals are very careful to assess how their capacities will stand up to the penalties for political activism, and that this tends to produce what she calls hybrid regimes, "governments that display both democratic and authoritarian tendencies."[29] But in these hybrids it is the state that is on top. It is cheering to realize that civil society not only exists but has a future in the state's own interest; but it is also true that in the dialectic of crackdown and easing that has marked Eurasia since 1993, "civil society" has had mainly a virtual role to play. It is a factor, but mainly in the imagination of elites. It is today's elites who may or may not call it into being as they fight each other to keep or gain power.

II

Politics as Elite Infighting

"Of shoes—and ships—and sealing-wax . . . "
Lewis Carroll

If civil society is anemic across the post-Soviet space, what does that do to the area's politics? The answer is that politics comes to consist largely in struggle among factions in the elites, groups in entrenched or competitive positions within existing power structures. To some extent politics is like that everywhere, including the United States. But politics is particularly a preserve of elites in the post-Soviet countries of the world.

Politics seemed much more wide open in the early years after the dissolution of the USSR. It was not just that millions of people were taking to the streets: it was also a time when every new country endowed itself with a hopeful parliament and when political parties proliferated. This had little to do with direct Western inspiration. As I noted in the first chapter, in those years Western assistance programs concentrated on humanitarian help and economic reform, with civil society and the rule of law lower priorities, and political development—such as party building and election monitoring—far behind.

It is true that there was a desperate aspiration to be Western, as a lifeline out of post-Soviet miseries, economic, moral, and political. That aspiration included democratic politics. Communism had lost the Cold War, and as in Central Europe after 1918 there was an urge to fill the spaces that defeat had left behind with the ideals and structures of the victors. And just as Central Europe had a decade of parliamentary democracy after 1918, the West's liberal democratic politics had great appeal again after 1991. Technically and politically, moreover, democratic political forms—elections and parliaments—are easier to introduce than market economics.[1] For all these reasons, the democratic impulse seemed natural after the fall.

Two major drags on the impulse became apparent quite early on, however. First, the post-Communist political class was overwhelmingly post-Soviet: the bulk of its members had come of age and learned their political inclinations and habits in the Soviet system. Second, as an ideological replacement for Soviet Communism, the nation-state was everywhere surprisingly weak.[2]

There had been no room at all in the Soviet Union for the rise of creative counterelites on the East Central European model. Soviet dissent had been successfully contained. No Solidarity arose to join workers and intellectuals in politics. No Charter 77 arose among the intelligentsia. The late Soviet Union had had peasant and worker and housewives' riots, but no sustained oppositional politics. Rioters were crushed or bought off, leaving no footprint in the political structure. Ethnic clashes had begun before the dissolution, between Armenians and Azeris in the Caucasus, between Kyrgyz and Uzbeks in the Ferghana Valley in Central Asia. But until dissolution came, such clashes were "merely" pogroms: they had no crystallized political content. The same could be said even of the high-level political contestation that was permitted at Union level in the last Gorbachev years: the infighting between fellow Party stalwarts Yegor Ligachev and Boris Yeltsin, from 1987 on, the campaigning for the new Congress of Peoples' Deputies in 1989.

To be sure, the limits on political activity were also purposeful: contestation was modest because it was the only kind allowed. In fact it was so modest, and it was allowed over so brief a period, that there was no chance for alternative elites to take shape. Those on whom freedom and independence devolved in 1991 were products of the system that had dissolved. Georgia's inflammatory first president Zviad Gamzakhurdia, for example, had been a dissident under the Soviets, but he was also the son of (Soviet) Georgia's most honored novelist; his successor Eduard Shevardnadze had been Soviet Foreign Minister, and before that Georgia's interior minister. In the five new Central Asian countries, four new Presidents had been Republic Party First Secretaries. Everything was up in the air, it seemed, except the new-old people in charge.

In fairness, there were some new openings for upward mobility into the elites during those early years. Data from 2001 show there was new room for new individuals, even for new leaders, who were still usually second-level members of the elite moving up.[3] The bureaucracy was more adhesive. That same year upwards of three-fifths of Russian second-tier and regional bureaucrats had been hired since 1990, but "Remarkably . . . every second federal employee at the central level was a holdover from the Brezhnev era."[4] Abulfaz Elchibey in Azerbaijan had been a professor of Middle East cultures; Askar Akayev in Kyrgyzstan had been a nuclear physicist working in Leningrad; in Belarus, Aleksandr Lukashenka had been a collective-farm chairman. So the old power structures were not all dismantled. But they were all demoralized, more open to new ways of doing things, to pressures from outside. Working in Poland and reading the 1992 Russian publication of documents proving that Stalin himself had authorized the 1940 massacres of Polish officers at Katyń, I thought such a revelation could not have happened before. (It probably could not happen today, in 2008.) There were other novelties. The media opened up. Privatization in the economy permitted not only new forms of owner-ship but new property owners. Elections became competitive, sometimes fiercely competitive. All these changes compelled those competing for political leadership to reach out beyond the narrow circles that had decided things before, to seek new, broader bases of support in society.

The ideology of governance, the justifications for rule, were also up in the air. The old system had not trained up many believers in democracy, but what it *had* trained up by way of people and attitudes often did not seem very useful or competitive in the trying new circumstances.

The Communist system in the Soviet Union and East Central Europe had operated like the American big-city machine in its heyday. Ideology was surcharged only on Election Day (or in the Soviet case on anniversaries) or in times of crisis. The quotidian reality consisted in the daily grinding of gigantic patronage structures dispensing goods and services and favors in return for support, or acquiescence, or loyalty, with maybe some payoffs on both sides. The guideline was the old Chicago formula: nobody gets nothing, nobody gets everything, everybody gets something.[5]

The system even had its own version of the ethnically balanced ticket, Federally and in the republics. Even though it was national in form, however, it was not national in content. Nor was this just because it was antinationalist in its goals, creating national forms precisely in order to control and eventually supersede nationalist content. It was also because Communist Party hegemony sapped the state structures in which it operated. The Soviet state and even the state structures it created in the federal Union were formally very strong, endowed with great powers. They even derived a certain emotional content from the tremendous joint victory in World War II, the Great Fatherland War. But their capacity to serve as vehicles in which nationalism could grow and create nation-states in the future was systematically vitiated by party primacy.

The proof came in the years of high struggle following the dissolution. It was a real crisis for sitting Soviet elites when the Soviet state dissolved into its constituent substates and the Party disappeared. Through the exit, Party and state took with them many of the resources that had been available to build and maintain the critical patronage networks on which leadership depended. The immediate reaction was for local power elites to grab at those resources that were left, withhold them from the center and use them for their own purposes. Privatization then removed even more resources from the elites' control. And the scramble for resources that ensued was terribly urgent: it was a crisis, but it also *felt* like a crisis. It was a time for quick decisions, taken without much reflection or ideological justification. They were decisions shaped by habit rather than ideals or even goals.

Almost every political action, it was true, could be justified in the name of welfare (which everyone understood) and in the name of stability, which was needed to ensure welfare (as everyone also understood). But with production and incomes declining and the social safety net shredding, welfare was in a tailspin and there was no stability. So there was also a need to broaden the ideological base for legitimate rule.

Where local elites turned for new ideological material varied a lot. "Sovereignty" was the great political issue of the very early years, from the dissolution of 1991 to mid-1993. Declarations of sovereignty vis-à-vis Moscow proliferated, both in the non-Russian republics and within Russia. In many places it was tempting to use ethnic-based nationalism as a weapon in the fight for sovereignty.[6]

Where nationalism was broad and deep, as in the Baltic republics, the notion of "sovereignty" led straight to independence. Elsewhere things were much more up in the air. Russia's Tatarstan is perhaps the most striking example, the most dangerous and the most instructive.

Tatarstan is oil-rich, and while Tatars had good positions within the political apparatus in Soviet times, they had fewer than Russians in the economy, and this made Tatar national separatism appealing among middling Tatar people who aspired to rise higher. But Yeltsin's Moscow proved willing to negotiate and accommodate, even to the extent of signing a power-sharing treaty with Tatarstan in 1994. That in turn gave Tatar moderates under President Mintimer Shaimiyev control of resources that they used to open the economy to Tatars, and this allowed them to outbid their separatist competitors politically. By mid-decade the Tatarstan that nationalist mobilization had threatened to tear from the Federation was witnessing nationalist demobilization and heading toward a new political stability based on good old-fashioned ethnic balancing by a good old-fashioned machine.[7]

Tatarstan showed that ethnic nationalism could wane as well as wax even in greenhouse conditions, far from any Western option. Since it is geographically far from the West, there was never a chance that the Tatar Republic would actually join the West or even secure international recognition for separation from Russia. Such options seemed more plausible in republics and regions geographically closer to the West. But there, paradoxically, that very plausibility created an equally effective antidote to ethnic nationalism: the postwar West they wanted to join disapproved of ethnic nationalism ideologically, and now in the 1990s the West was also getting bruised on ethnic nationalism's bloody knuckles in the Balkans, and was eager to help contain the monster farther east.

So beginning in 1994, the West gave concrete form to the option of "joining the West" in the countries closest to it by holding out the prospect of NATO and EU enlargement, with a stately series of conditionalities concerning liberal democratic governance. Where the option was most plausible, in the Baltic republics, this factor was the most decisive for taming ethnic nationalism and putting it in a "European" framework that defined citizenship in civic rather than ethnic terms, as both NATO and EU entry required. Once Baltic progress into European structures gained momentum, it allowed the three republics to manage not only their very real economic dependencies on their eastern neighbors but also the extremely hard issues of sovereignty, citizenship and rights for minorities that they had inherited from the Soviet Union, Russian in the case of Latvia and Estonia, Polish in the case of Lithuania. The nationalisms of the Baltic "titular" ethnic majorities—Estonian, Latvian, Lithuanian—are powerful, so the work of taming is never done, as was shown once again in the 2007 flare-up between Estonia and Russia over Estonia's moving the monument to World War II Soviet soldiers from the center of Tallinn. But by 2008 all three republics had become so "European" that their main issues will seldom overlap with those of this book.

Even after the West had opened the door a crack in 1994, however, "joining the West" was not a reliable political option for post-Soviet countries outside the Baltic republics. Western connections that might thicken into hope were still quite thin. Actual aid flows were relatively small. To take but one example, the $2.5 billion in bilateral assistance provided by the U.S. Congress in 1993 amounted to just about $10 per capita across the post-Soviet space. Even at those levels Western aid had uncertain staying power in donor-country budgets; and it gave uncertain staying power to incumbents in countries turning upside down. The Chinese proverb that Chou En-lai had been fond of quoting in his day applied now: "Distant waters do not put out fires." And the more distant a country was from the West, the less plausible a lifeline Western aid became. In the most critical early years Western humanitarian assistance kept Armenia and Georgia alive, and it was very important in Kyrgyzstan, nestled in Central Asia's mountains among China, Uzbekistan, Kazakhstan, and war-ridden Tajikistan. But there was never enough Western assistance to lever settlement of any of the new regional conflicts in the USSR's old borderlands, never enough to lift Armenia, or Georgia, or Kyrgyzstan beyond the status of countries with a few million people and few resources, gripped by turmoil.

If the West fell short as savior or patron, so did new ties with new neighbors, but not for lack of effort. Post-Soviet successor states joined every international organization that was willing, and they also multiplied new groupings of their own. This joining was driven partly by economics, by the need to maintain or recreate as many of the economic connections that had linked them in the integrated Soviet economy, even after Russia scrapped its ruble zone experiment in 1993, while they reached out for more efficient partners elsewhere. But the motivation was also political: Russia, destined by geography and its resources to be the center of any new constellation, was a necessary partner for every other new independent state, and Russia was an enthusiastic promoter of new forms of partnership. Even though it was on the strategic defensive, even though it was politically up in the air, Russia was involved militarily and politically in each of the new regional conflicts. Many of its troops and bases and facilities remained in place. Between 1992 and 1997 Tajikistan descended into bloody civil war, with Russia supporting one side, and its porous border with Afghanistan was defended by Russian troops. The evacuation plan of the American Embassy in Dushanbe called for personnel to be taken to the airport by the 201st Russian Motorized Rifle Division, and the plan was duly executed in 1992. The Embassy was back in the Tajikistan Hotel by the time I visited the next spring, but the Russian Embassy was on the floor below, and we were all protected by Russian Special Purpose Forces (Spetsnaz). Somehow Russian presences did not seem as imperial close up as they might have from far away.[8]

Yet of course the hegemonic impulse and fear of it remained alive and well, if in the background for the time being. Paradoxically again, the breakup of the Soviet Union and the new Russia's weakness merely invigorated the discourse on empire that had arisen in the Soviet Union's late years.[9] Then local elites had feared successful assimilation into a Soviet polity with a new "Soviet" culture. Now they were liberated from direct Moscow rule but feared its reimposition. So the discourse on Russian imperialism was fueled not just by Russian presences but also by a healthy respect for Russia's size and potential. No one wanted to be on the wrong side of a resurgent

Russia, if it came to that. So accommodation was a constant accompaniment to the vigorous suspicion and paranoia—outside Russia about Russian intentions, inside Russia about everyone else's—that sprang up in the USSR's ruins. All were legacies of the Soviet Union's odd, not-quite-imperial character.

Formally, accommodation produced a plethora of organizations. Some were limited to post-Soviet states, others extended to countries outside. They were hard to keep track of even for participants: the Commonwealth of Independent States (CIS); the Shanghai Five, later the Shanghai Cooperation Organization (SCO); the Single Economic Space (SES); the Collective Security Treaty Organization (CSTO); the Eurasian Economic Community (EURASEC) and the Central Asian Cooperation Organization (CACO), which later merged under the former name;[10] GUUAM, comprising Georgia, Ukraine, Uzbekistan, Azerbaijan and Moldova, later reduced to GUAM by Uzbekistan's departure;[11] the Community of Democratic Choice, founded in December 2005 to bring Ukraine and Georgia together after their color revolutions along with Romania, Moldova, the three Baltic republics, Macedonia and Slovenia, but evidently meeting seldom since then. The CIS has had its checkered career but subsists; it figures in bilateral bargaining between Russia and neighbors who occasionally threaten to leave it, and it has probably cushioned Russia's early post-Soviet geostrategic decline.[12]

But integration within Eurasia was still part of the Russian foreign minister Sergei Lavrov's agenda for 2008: "If we put aside the various phobias, all the 12 member countries have common interests." Lavrov was also clear about the reasons: "We have understandable, legitimate, explicit, and transparent interests in the post-Soviet region, but we intend to realize these interests through cooperation based on mutual respect and mutual benefit."[13] Since 9/11 the SCO, which includes China as well as Russia and the Central Asian states, has taken on some international consistency. It has been the vehicle for much good work delimiting new international borders, and in July 2005 it was the SCO that "invited" a U.S. timetable for ending use of Central Asian bases. Some economic organizations have facilitated modestly useful steps on issues like trade and standards. Overall, however, none of these new bodies compared in substance and effect with the great Western organizations they tried to impress. Russian leaders have promoted CSTO ties with NATO in vain,[14] and although some CSTO links supplemented the crucial bilateral ties between agencies and factions, it is these latter that remain the heart of political relations within the region. Post-Soviet Eurasia today is still what the English economist Peter Wiles once called the Stalinist socialist commonwealth in its heyday: a wheel with enormous spokes (running to Moscow) and scarcely any rim.[15]

It is bilateral access to Moscow agencies and factions that still matters most. But it is also true that unlike Stalin's Russia, the Russian Federation of the 1990s was confused as an entity and as an international actor. Vis-à-vis its new neighbors it was certainly not a seedbed of democratization; but it was not precisely *undemocratic* either. Even after Yeltsin suppressed the rambunctious parliament and got a presidentialist constitution by referendum in 1993, even after his regime became presidentialist in practice as well as in form with the passage of time, even after it plunged into the war in Chechnya in 1994, Russia still had competitive politics, with genuine choices, as in the presidential election of 1996. There was still some freedom of expression and assembly; there was a range of economic actors; some modern institutions were introduced and consolidated. It was not Russia, therefore, that drove its post-Soviet partners toward authoritarian rule. Russia may not have discouraged the trend, but it was domestic politics in the other countries that created it.

Several factors, some of them overlapping, were pushing them toward authoritarianism. At least since Stalin's death the Kremlin had always been respectful of regional power centers. The Soviet Union's version of balanced tickets could be ethnically based, as in Central Asia and the Caucasus, or it could be simply regional: Leonid Brezhnev's southwest Ukrainian Dnipropetrovs'k group was one core of leadership politicking in the 1950s and 1960s, like Andrei Kirilenko's West Siberians in the 1970s. With the USSR gone, local leaders now hunkered down within their home networks with a vengeance. Their lifelines were not to the West but into the centers of their own worlds.

Rooting into home ground came most naturally in the war zones where ethnic or regional passions were part of the struggle. Tajikistan's civil war pitted regions against each other before it reached down to clans and up to a universalist ideology, in this case Islamism. In the Caucasus, strongman rule had been traditional both north and south of the Russian border, balancing and unifying tribes and clans that were otherwise perpetually at each other's throats. The pressures of war reinforced the appeal of strongmen, and that produced (or reproduced) leaders like Heydar Aliyev in Azerbaijan and Robert Kocharyan in Armenia. "Sovereignty issues" retained a salience in the politics of war zones long after sovereignty had been subsumed in the struggle for resources elsewhere. Strongman rule did not therefore abolish political contestation. But it substantially confined political contest within the elite. More and more, the democratic or parliamentary forms introduced after the Soviet collapse came to serve as signals or indicators of how things were going in elite infighting.

Outside the war zones—and most of the post-Soviet space in fact was not in war zones—the trend was toward presidentialism, which scholars have parsed into a number of varieties: plain or "super" or "hyper." Beginning in 1993 in Russia and then in country after country, parliaments were neutered, presidential terms were extended, and presidential authorities were reinforced. The one exception has been Moldova, which has developed a genuine mixed presidential-parliamentary form of governance even though it is torn by civil conflict with its Russian-speaking Trans-Dniestria district, which operates as a kind of thug republic under the strongman Igor Smirnov. Elsewhere, presidential rule has come to be the rule.[16] It has proved the best way—the most familiar and most efficient way—to organize the struggle of elites for survival, for position, for primacy. It has generally gotten stronger over time, and even developed a mini-ideology of its own.

In Russia, Central Asia, and the Caucasus, pro-presidential parties surfaced in the new millennium to bolster presidential rule via the elections now required of all members of the international community in good standing. These parties come in somewhat different shapes and sizes. Uzbekistan's is more of a phalanx, say, than Azerbaijan's. With some muscle and some manipulation, United Russia swept the regional elections in March 2007, then took two-thirds of the parliamentary election vote in December under the leadership of the prime-minister-to-be, Putin, and then powered the practically uncontested election of Medvedev as his successor in March 2008. In Turkmenistan there is still only one party, led by Berdymukhammedov: hard to top. But in Kazakhstan presidentialism had a good year too. In February a "constitutional task force" endorsed the presidential system; in May President Nursultan Nazarbayev signed legislation lifting his term limits; in August his Nur Otan party won every seat in an expanded parliament. Kyrgyzstan's path was less smooth, as usual, if only because there has been a tug of war over presidential and parliamentary powers ever since the Tulip Revolution of 2005, and moves to increase presidential power can still be overturned in court. And so it happened in 2007: the pro-government Ak-Jol party won every single seat in the December 16 parliamentary elections but was then forced to shoehorn four more small parties into parliament by a court order invalidating an over-clever election rule.[17]

Presidential rule also needs to be justified, and that too is happening. Kazakhstan's President Nazarbayev wants Kazakhstan to be "a respected, liberal, and democratic state," but clearly believes only presidential rule can get it there. His area example is Ukraine: the Orange Revolution of 2004 shifted power from the president to parliament, but "when the parliament started using its powers, the president started having representative capacity only —like the Queen in the UK"—he could not become the guarantor of stability, and "started claiming his powers back." Kyrgyzstan is now going the same way. "Do we need it?" Nazarbayev asked, and quoted Charles de Gaulle to the effect that rule by political parties brought France's collapse. Putin and his associates are also fond of analogy, this time to the New Deal. The deputy administration head Vladislav Surkov argued last February that "like Roosevelt during his presidency, Putin has to consolidate administrative control and use presidential power to the maximum to overcome a crisis." In October Putin put it this way: "In the years when the United States was coming out of the Great Depression, much was done 'manually,' which part of the elite did not like. But the results of that were that the United States emerged from the crisis, which benefited the elite and all the citizens of the country." Dmitry Medvedev can sound even more like a democrat than Nazarbayev. He has said and repeated that Russia is building a democracy "without unnecessary additional qualifications" (this a swipe at Surkov's "sovereign democracy" concept, of which more later); that citizen involvement is essential; that "freedom is better than non-freedom." But he is also at least as adamant about the

need for a firm presidential hand on the tiller: "If Russia is turned into a parliamentary republic, it will disappear."[18]

Bulking up presidential rule with beefy new parties is supposed to make it stronger, and that may be happening. But it is important to ask why the effort is being made. What is it these presidents are trying harder to control? For this is not the Soviet situation. In Turkmenistan's capital, Ashgabat, in the fall of 2006 I watched a rehearsal for the celebration of the fifteenth anniversary of independence that was to be performed for "Turkmenbashi" Niyazov the next week. The massed columns of bureaucrats and workers lumbering on cue around the central square were so reminiscent of the May Days and Revolution Days of my diplomatic youth that I had to do a double take. But the reality is in fact different, and different almost everywhere in Eurasia.

Often there is still some political competition, even if increasingly contrived; there are still some liberties and freedoms; there are now many market features in the economy. Many of these states are after all weak, and that means they have limited resources even for repression. As I shall describe in the next chapter, much of the political struggle is indeed about access to those resources, since they are the lifeblood of the patronage networks that provide the structure of politics. This has led to what Lucan Way has dubbed rapacious individualism, as practice and as ideology, a kind of energetic Hobbesian acquisitiveness. In another paradox, however, this "rapacious individualism" has had the effect of limiting whatever

dictatorial tendencies drive individual leaders.[19] Those limits, moreover, were often reinforced by the leader's desire to keep the country in good odor with the international community, to keep aid flowing, to maintain political support or acquiescence, or just to hedge against Russian hegemonism.

Steven Levitsky and Lucan Way have also coined another useful term for this new brand of post-Soviet rule: "competitive authoritarianism."[20] Outside the war zones, however, it has taken two main forms—East and West— which tell us what today's "presidentializers" are up against.

In the East, leaders or competitors for leadership have tended to reach back to traditional clan loyalties to anchor and secure their rule. Those loyalties sometimes had a religious component, as they had for Tajikistan's Islamic Renaissance Party, and as they have come to have in Chechnya. In the North Caucasus the local tribes and clans had resisted Russian rule for decades in the mid-nineteenth century, and as the guerrilla war ground on year after year, more and more of them looked to Islam to subsume their divisions and give them the unity they needed to keep fighting. Their leader Imam Shamil was a sheikh of the Naqshbandi Sufi order. Sufism in Islam is generally quietistic and apolitical (and the Naqshbandis in particular are historically famous for their capacity to get along with governments). In the Caucasus war, however, it turned slowly into something else. And in our time Russia's two Chechnya wars (1994–1996 and since 1999) have had the same result. What began as a Chechen national separatist struggle has become more and more religious, more and more universalist and more and more murderous in its ideology.[21]

In most of Central Asia and the Caucasus, however, the clan loyalties on which politics was being rebased did not have a pronounced religious component. The Chechens and the Gharm Valley fighters in Tajikistan are the exception, not the rule. It is important to understand "clan" broadly in any case. Even when they are built on blood ties, these political groupings very often accrete members based on regional origin or common schooling or simply personal loyalty, all bound together by common interest. Probably the German term *Seilschaften,* roped groups of climbers on a sheer mountain face, describes them best. In that sense, the security types whom Putin has made great in Russian governance are a "clan" too. In Central Asia and the Caucasus, however, kinship is more likely to be the foundation and the glue.

That is not to say that clan loyalties cannot be more or less attenuated by wealth. As more resources become available, the struggle for access to them may become less savage, less needful of primordial passion to sustain itself. We have seen something of the sort under way in Russia's Tatarstan; it could also be a factor in Kazakhstan, with its growing oil wealth, or we could see the same evolution in Turkmenistan, with its revenues from natural gas (if Turkmenistan developments become less opaque). In all these countries, however, including Armenia and Georgia with their Christian populations, the "big men" who govern pay careful attention to clan balancing even if it is masked as balancing among regions. And instead of stoking ethnic nationalism, clan balancing helps them keep on top of it. They are indeed trying to build states, but with ideologies that are still subnational.[22]

Further west, in Russia and Ukraine, leaders still pay very careful attention to their regions, and of course Moldova's president, Vladimir Voronin, can just not get away from his Trans-Dniestria and its Russian-speaking mafiosi rulers. But in the large republics with mainly Slav populations, in what was the Soviet heartland, regionalism is much less kinship-based than it is to the east and south.

Ethnic consciousness is pervasive, to be sure. Yet what is striking is not how much but how little ethnic nationalism it generates, and how little conflict among the various ethnic groups. In the early years tension existed, and was even high, say between Ukrainians and Russians in Ukraine's Crimea. More recently the cleavages that Ukraine's Orange Revolution opened up between its Ukrainian-speaking west and the Russian-speaking east have prompted new fears, and even more recently the issue of making Russian a state language became a football on Ukraine's political gridiron.[23] Yet Moldova is the only post-Soviet country bordering on Europe where actual fighting broke out, in the very special circumstances of 1992, and even there the cease-fire negotiated in 1994 has generally held. Perhaps Trans-Dniestria served as a warning to the other peoples of the post-Soviet west Eurasia. Perhaps proximity to Europe also helped, even if Europe at the time was a Romania that had helped spark the fighting and entered the European Union only years later, in 2007.

Whatever the reasons, all these countries resolutely define citizenship in civic rather than ethnic terms, and all work hard to make civic citizenship a reality. In the most confused situation, in Ukraine, ethnic divisions are very clear, and polling data show them becoming clearer with time, yet they have not (or not yet) taken on decisive political significance. State-consciousness based on regions appears to have sealed these countries off from virulent ethnic nationalism as surely as clan loyalties have in the Caucasus and Central Asia.

What Russia and Ukraine have instead of clans are oligarchs. Post-Soviet oligarchs are creations of the state, since their wealth derives from privatized state property, but they are not necessarily creatures of the state. They come in various sizes and shapes. Generally their wealth is sectoral. In Russia it derives mainly from oil and gas, nickel, gold, and diamonds; in Ukraine it is more broadly based (and smaller, since Ukraine has fewer exportable natural resources). But in both cases the post-Soviet state alienated huge chunks of what had been and what is still widely regarded as national patrimony to private individuals, and then depended for stable revenues on taxing them or confiscating some of the loot back.

The rise of economic oligarchy thus defined the post-Soviet politics of Russia and Ukraine, states that after all include four-fifths of Eurasia's post-Soviet population. Patronage networks were the main actors in politics and society; to maintain them resources were required which could only come from oligarchs; and this was the origin of Lucan Way's competitive authoritarianism.[24]

Presidentialism, then, is the post-Communist Eurasian state's answer to clans and oligarchs who had so much to do with creating that state in the first place. It is not a particularly attractive answer—we have seen how it needs to be justified—nor does it always establish secure primacy. I have noted how "clans" need to be broadly defined; "oligarchs," it turns out, need to be understood in much the same way: they are created by the state and knotted into it more tightly than the most ingratiating American defense contractor can imagine, but they are broader in origin and interests than any industry alone. And the deeper scholarship burrows into the real workings of these systems, the clearer it becomes that the real issue in their politics is whether the state can rise above its origins in society and economy. In the next chapter we shall see how the struggle has played out in Russia. But versions of it have been underway in Central Asia, the Caucasus, and even Belarus.

Whether the state is weak or strong, the impulse is the same. Tajikistan has been and Kyrgyzstan has become more like free-for-alls than national states, but in each country leaders strive for authority beyond the clan or regional constituencies who put them in power. Musclebound Uzbekistan has developed a neopatrimonialism that keeps all the regional power brokers and their patronage networks in motion, with only President Islom Karimov and his family above the fray. At the other end of Eurasia in Belarus, President Lukashenka has managed a similar feat, incessantly shuffling governors and enterprise heads to keep new power bases from forming. He too has a son, thirty-one-year-old Viktar, in training as supervisor of the country's security and law-enforcement agencies. The president may find, though, that family members sometimes need to be part of the shuffle too. That has certainly been Nazarbayev's experience in Kazakhstan: 2007 was not just the Year of the Strong Presidency, it was also the Year of the Sidelined Family, and surely the two were functionally related. As the semi-changing of the guard approached in Russia, there were hints and signs that Putin was distancing himself from the security professionals he had brought to power with him and enriched beyond belief, that is, his "clan." President-to-be Medvedev, it was noted, came from a different career path. Everywhere we see the same effort to keep power by building it out beyond and above family, clan, and oligarchy.[25]

This effort may not succeed in any given country, but it is what's coming down, as youth would have it, and it is also the explanation for the system's structural dynamic, what makes it change, what saves it from simple inertial extrapolation. The political scientist Henry Hale has pointed out that the patronal presidential regimes that became characteristic of the post-Soviet space in the mid-1990s generally remain stable so long as the patronage networks expect the leader to continue in power. Once the leader's longevity is subject to doubt, however, networks and their leaders begin to hedge and prepare for alternatives. This can happen either when the leader approaches legally mandated term limits or when he begins to appear too weak to extend his rule by changing the law or by electoral fraud.

All post-Soviet systems provide for elections of some kind (just as the Soviet system did), but unlike Soviet elections these serve today's elites as tests of the leader's intentions and staying power. Parliamentary elections often precede presidential elections and function as warm-ups. Public opinion is also important, as a harbinger of future electoral shifts. So is the technique of mass mobilization, passed like a torch among activists, from Serbia to Georgia to Ukraine to Kyrgyzstan, but usually flammable only after a clearly fraudulent election. So are independent or at least semiautonomous media that give accurate information that is not available from those under state control, and, even more, that provides a sense of the possibility of change.

The color revolutions that marched across the post-Soviet space between 2003 and 2005 were therefore multifaceted. Each began with electoral fraud and the mass reaction it produced, yet that was not the essential cause-and-effect sequence. Even more critical was their common starting point, in the leader's incapacity to prolong his grip on power, in the mounting conviction among elites that leadership change was in the offing and that a succession process had started, and the mounting struggle among them to be on the right side of any outcome. It was when Shevardnadze in Georgia and Leonid Kuchma in Ukraine and Akayev in Kyrgyzstan announced they would not succeed themselves that elements of their elites began to hedge and plot, to send funds abroad, to cultivate contacts in the "power agencies"—the police and army—which in each case refused to support the leader when crisis came.[26] Armenia in 2008 fits the pattern I see, since it was term limits for Robert Kocharyan that forced the election in question, and certainly the elite there is splitting. But at this writing the situation in the security forces is still unclear.[27] The masses are indeed important, but as auxiliaries: they are the infantry of armies led— and indeed created—by factions within the elite.[28]

Elite infighting over access to resources is thus the stuff of post-Soviet politics, but it produces both stability and upheavals. To understand why, we need to return to the complex interplay of economics and "sovereignty" across this new world region.

III

THE POLITICS OF ECONOMICS
AND SOVEREIGNTY

"Of cabbages—and kings . . . "
LEWIS CARROLL

If infighting among elites has been the stuff of politics
in the post-Soviet space, what do they fight about?

Deprived of the unifying ideology of Communism,
they no longer fight to end the exploitation of man by
man, nor to consolidate and improve "really existing socialism." They are not (or not yet) driven by nationalism
based on ethnocultural identities. So the natural answer
would be that post-Soviet elites fight about economics.
They fight over access to resources that were scarce to begin with and dwindled still further in the painful period
of retrenchment and readjustment that followed Communism's fall. Economies are now expanding again, but
the fight goes on: the fear of losing is always near. Fighting can be direct or indirect. Elite factions can struggle to
get and keep resources; they can struggle to define terms
of access to resources that are favorable to themselves.
In either case, the reason for fighting is that resources

are needed to keep together the patronage networks on which political power depends.

The payoffs can be very direct. In Turkmenistan, President Niyazov would promise Mercedeses to ministers "who work well in the cotton harvest"; regional and district governors who met production targets were to get jeeps. And if they did not perform, they got smacked.[1] In Russia's Chuchotka Autonomous Okrug, Governor Roman Abramovich was Russia's richest man for three years running, though he has now ceded the top spot to his fellow oligarch Oleg Deripaska, who started with Abramovich in aluminum but now has holdings in other metals, cars, and construction as well. As he anticipated selling his oil company to the giant state gas monopoly Gazprom in 2005, Abramovich ordered the world's largest yacht—160 meters long, worth $179 million—from a German shipyard; he already owned the world's fifth and sixth largest. In 2007 he became the first person to own a private Airbus 380, to add to his Boeing 737 and his Boeing 767.[2] And when former associates of the imprisoned oil magnate Mikhail Khodorkovsky turned on their ex-boss, they complained that he was "stingy"—that he took 60 percent of salary payments for himself and left only 7 percent each for them.[3] It is all very concrete.

Much of the rapacity in the politics of rapacious individualism is therefore about straight economic resources. Yet economics is never just economic. The *Homo economicus* of classical economics has never existed in nature. "Economics" is as much a feature of consciousness as any other feature of the social landscape, as "the nation," for instance, or "the individual." This has been as true in the post-Soviet space as elsewhere. In its actual political experience, economics has been thoroughly commingled with sovereignty issues. Yet the proportions shift over time as circumstances change. To an extent this is true across Eurasia; let us follow these shifting mixtures chronologically since the Soviet dissolution, with a special focus on the largest player, Russia.

1991–93: The Preeminence of Sovereignty

Economics and sovereignty were most intertwined in Eurasian politics in the early post-Soviet years, from 1991 to the summer of 1993. Two fine recent studies of the period show just how intimately.

In the beginning Russia tried to keep alive a ruble zone for most of the area, a zone in which Russia's currency would serve all the member states as well as Russia itself. The experiment proved costly and cumbersome, and Russia ditched it in 1993. But the business scholar Rawi Abdelal's close examination of the record shows that elites in post-Soviet countries that were likely to suffer most outside a ruble zone—namely, the Baltic Republics—were nevertheless the most eager to get out of the zone, while elites in countries that were benefiting least from inclusion—in Central Asia—were the most willing to stay in. The key variable driving policy approaches, Abdelal finds, was not "objective" economic interest but *nationalism,* strongest in the Baltics and weakest in Central Asia.[4]

Similarly, the political economist Yoshiko Herrera finds that objective economic factors do not explain the very different political trajectories of two major Russian regions, Sverdlovsk and Saratov, in these years. Although the two regions were very similar in structure and economic performance, Sverdlovsk politics was dominated by a sense of economic injustice at the hands of Moscow, a feeling that was practically absent in Saratov, and in Sverdlovsk it issued into political support for a separatist Urals Republic. Here the struggle for resources was defined politically by economic imagination, in conjunction with specific political and institutional circumstances. When the circumstances changed, after 1993, so did imaginations, and the Urals Republic faded from the political agenda.[5]

Yet while sovereignty issues can define economic issues, the explosion of sovereignty movements and declarations across the post-Soviet space in these years very often had an economic subtext. Demands for sovereignty was often "about" access to economic resources. To take the example of Russia's Tatarstan again, middle-level Tatars were attracted to separatism as a way of remedying perceived job discrimination by Russians, and once prosperity, privatization, and local control opened new job opportunities for them, separatism faded. In region after region, the name of the game was to keep resources from Moscow in order to use them locally, but it was called a struggle for "sovereignty."[6]

1993–98: The Preeminence of Economics

By the mid-1990s, the "sovereignty" wave was actually ebbing everywhere except in some of the war zones around Russia's fringes, where the wars kept it alive. Despite cease-fires in mid-decade, sovereignty continued (and continues) to be a burning issue in Moldova's Trans-Dniestria, in and around Nagorno-Karabakh, in two of Georgia's now-frozen conflicts. Agitation for sovereignty has not been so central in Tajikistan, because regional tensions inflected by clan and ideology still dominate as they dominated during the civil war of 1992–97; and in Chechnya such subnational issues have been morphing into an ethnonationalism for Russians and a Huntingtonian "clash of civilizations" for Chechens. Each is nasty; neither is typical.

Outside the war zones, however, after 1993 sovereignty and other grander goals faded as objects of political struggle and gave way to brutal competition for economic resources without much in the way of ideological dignity, to rapacity without benefit of clergy, as the British used to say. Politically and socially, there was a general settling down and settling in. Migrations slowed; presidential regimes became the rule; oligarchs and clans emerged as their creators, counterparts, and competitors. In Russia the Yeltsin regime put in place institutional devices—the Constitution of 1993, the Federation Council, governors—for regularizing political and economic contestation and pursuing it without violence. Yet economies were still in crises that seemed endless; if they were stabilizing it was at lower levels; social security had been blown away. In Russian politics, fear of disintegration receded, but the economy looked hopelessly mired in inflation, contraction, and misery for most. In most of Russia and for most of its post-Soviet neighbors, grabbing and holding on to resources in order to sustain patronage networks became the content of politics.

The struggle for resources had an international form that depended a great deal on the resources each country had. Countries with exportable resources wanted Western help to exploit them. That included Kazakhstan and Azerbaijan, which were rich in oil; Turkmenistan, which was rich in natural gas; and Russia, which was rich in both. In all of them, commodity exports provided between a fifth and one half of the GDP; this was true when oil was at $20 a barrel, in the early 1990s, as it has remained true through the subsequent oil market boom. In all these countries, government revenues—what the state needs to run—depended to an extraordinary degree on energy exports.

In this situation, Russia needed revenues from oil and gas sales, but it also wanted to maintain its monopoly over transit routes to market that it had inherited from the Soviet Union. The result was to kick off a decade and a half of intricate and bad-tempered Caspian Basin pipeline diplomacy involving not just the littoral countries (including Russia) but also the West, with its markets and its investment resources for rehabilitation of the old .pipelines (and production facilities) and construction of new ones. This is a story that continues today, and I will follow some of its ups and downs in the chapter's later sections. The point here is that struggles over oil and gas production and transport have marked post-Soviet Eurasia's political experience from the beginning, simply because of the region's extraordinary economic dependence on energy.

The struggle for resources was even more intense in domestic politics. Leaders had neither the time nor the energy to formulate great goals for themselves or their countries; they were fighting too hard just to survive. And while there was some settling down between 1993 and 1998, it left in place many of the old structures and the old ways of doing things. Prices of basic commodities were still widely subsidized, even in international trade: Russia sold its oil and gas to post-Soviet partners at far below world market prices, and the same was true of the water rising in Kyrgyzstan's and Tajikistan's mountains in Central Asia: without a price under the Soviets, water had kept the downstream cotton fields in Uzbekistan and Turkmenistan going, and it is still without a price because the Uzbeks and Turkmen refuse to pay one. There was some rejuvenation of elites, as noted in the last chapter, but new people melded into the Soviet-style networks that were still vital to the operation of economies and governments, perhaps even more vital as property was privatized. With nothing else to go on—for there were no strong political parties—states were still weak.

In the mid-1990s, therefore, politics was "about" economics; familiar networks fought to get and keep and exclude their rivals from access to goods. Something of that brand of politics persists today in the annual negotiations over gas prices and transit fees between states like Russia and Turkmenistan, which have gas, and states like Ukraine and Belarus, which do not. Elites in the former negotiate from positions of some strength, elites in the latter from positions of some weakness. In these underinstitutionalized systems, however, these elites are as likely to be in cahoots with each other as loyal to their new national governments when decisions loom. Among many other factors, that helps explain why these famous confrontations seem suddenly to end in opaque arrangements involving mysterious partners that succeed no one knows how.[7] In the mid-1990s that was very much the style of politics in general across Eurasia. It showed how weak these new states were. Today, a decade later, the annual opera of gas negotiations seems a little old-fashioned, even a little quaint, because the interpenetration of elites is ceasing to be typical. And it is ceasing to be typical because politics, economics and the states that manage them have changed so much in the interim. States may not entirely rule this piece of mankind, but in most of Eurasia they are in the saddle.

1998–2005: The "Liberal Empire"

Nineteen ninety-eight was the key year for getting them there, the year the shape of the typical Eurasian political game changed in basic ways: *eppur si muove*—"and yet it does move," as Galileo murmured about the earth as he left the courtroom. And the reason was that politics about economics placed extraordinary political burdens on the region's largest country, Russia. Partly this was because of Russia's sheer comparative size, partly because Russia carries so much of the Soviet Union's ambiguous imperial legacy. In the post-Soviet space the discourse of empire—whether or not Russia is or wishes to be imperial and how much and at what cost—is simply an unavoidable fact of life. Yet that discourse has no necessary term:

since the data are always so ambiguous, it need never end. If it comes to conclusions, it is for specific reasons, as a result of identifiable cause-and-effect processes in the lives of states and economies. And in the 1990s the specific reason pushing the discourse to reboot was that Russia's dependence on oil and gas exports for state revenues meant that the Russian state could function and consolidate itself after the throes of transition only if the newly created Russian oligarchs were willing to pay a fair share of taxes.

And in the 1990s they were not. They were willing to pitch in during the presidential election of 1996 and provide the resources that brought Boris Yeltsin from single-digit approval ratings to a second term, in return for chunks of state property lopped off for them under an arrangement known as "loans for shares." But 1996 was a one-shot; in general the Russian oligarchs withheld their taxes, so that the Russian economy remained chaotic, the Russian state remained ineffective, and as Yeltsin's own performance deteriorated, more and more Russians came to associate a privatized economy with Russian state weakness, with the international dole—for international financial institutions proved extraordinarily willing to carry this debilitated economy forward despite that debility—and with national humiliation. So when the Russian state defaulted on its debts in 1998, "sovereignty" issues returned to take their revenge on the politics-as-grab-and-hold that had superseded them in mid-decade.

The 1998 economic crisis provided a respite. It frightened both Yeltsin's state and Russia's oligarchs enough to drive them into a new modus vivendi: the state would allow the oligarchs to keep their ill-gotten gains, and the oligarchs would pay their fair share of taxes and stay out of politics.[8]

The aftermath of crisis also coincided with major political change. Vladimir Putin became prime minister in the summer of 1999 just as Chechen rebels attacked the neighboring Russian Caucasus republic of Dagestan. Putin renewed a war in Chechnya that had been in abeyance since 1996, and the resulting popular approval helped underpin the deal he struck to replace Yeltsin that New Year's Eve 2000, a deal ratified by the voters the next spring. Putin brought to Russian politics a new mood of self-assertion and confidence, which could be felt in area after area of governance and economic life.

Since confidence permits retreat as well as advance, it is not paradoxical that Caspian Basin pipeline diplomacy subsided a bit at the end of the decade, when a consensus emerged among the contenders in favor of multiple routes for oil: rehabilitated older pipelines, a Russian-dominated Caspian Pipeline Consortium pipeline from Kazakhstan to the Russian Black Sea port of Novorossiysk, completed in 2001, and a Baku-Tbilisi-Ceyhan (Turkey) pipeline with heavy American participation that delivered its first oil to market in 2006. And when the September 11 crisis broke in 2001, Putin handled it with the same sure-footedness: his choice of joining the U.S. in the Global War on Terrorism had to be forced on parts of his government, but there was a payoff in an international semibye for Russia's Chechnya policy along with a new international respect and equality for Russia, all of which served to balance the increased U.S. military presence in Central Asia. By early 2002 Putin and President Bush were hammering out a new "strategic partnership," to general applause. Russia was indeed on a comeback trail.

The question was where the new-old Putin regime wanted this trail to lead, what it would do with its new confidence and new resources at home and abroad. For a long time the answer was very unclear; it is still not entirely clear today. Suspicion about Russia's real aims is a legacy of the Soviet Union to the other populations of the post-Soviet world as well as to us, and we should be cautious in our judgments for just that reason. Transparency is not a strong feature of Russian governance; intentions are often hard to deduce from actions, and contingency drives things there, too. When the outside world tries to parse Russian actions and intentions it should keep an eye out for honest confusion.

Looking back, though, we can see the basic idea that was already in place in Russia in those years: Russian state interests and Russian economic assets are interdependent, and should be mutually supporting. Here too caution is called for: in the late 1940s it took two years and a succession of crises before the main prescriptions of George Kennan's "long telegram" of 1946 became U.S. policy. The time for an idea does not come until it comes, as Yogi Berra might put it. But policy usually does not come without ideas, and from the mid-1990s on there existed a strong conviction in Russia that the debility of the state could be ascribed to the unnatural transfer to private individuals of state property that was national patrimony. And it came just as "naturally" to believe that the way to restore the authority of the state was for the state to recover and wield these economic assets. Where the do mestic economy was concerned, surely, the concept of "verticality"—restoration of the state through replacement of the horizontal dispersion of power under Yeltsin by hierarchical authority emanating from top to bottom —was there from the beginning of Putin's administration.

Deep in the cacophony of Russian governance a bell began to toll on oligarchy. Boris Berezovsky had been one of the greatest of the oligarchs. He had been close to the Yeltsin administration and was one of Putin's original sponsors; by 2000 he was an immensely rich airline and media magnate (in his latest avatars). He had also begun to finance liberal politics. He was not invited to the Kremlin in July 2000 when the newly elected Putin met with twenty-one oligarchs and reaffirmed that if they stayed out of politics they could keep their money. After Putin then blew up at Berezovsky over the way his media covered the tragic explosion of the nuclear submarine *Kursk*, Berezovsky sold his TV shares to Abramovich, who later passed them on to the state, and then left in October for London, where he lives in political asylum to this day.[9]

The use of Russia's economic assets to leverage the wider world was not absent either. As part of their strategic partnership Presidents Bush and Putin announced a new energy dialogue at their May 2002 summit, and the meetings that followed were hopeful about large long-term energy cooperation, including Russian gas and even oil supplies; some Americans looked to (non-OPEC) Russian oil as a counterweight to OPEC on the world pricing scale. But Russia was coming from so far back that at the outset it was more plausible for it to make use of its economic leverage on its "near abroad"—its newly sovereign Eurasian neighbors.

The concept of a new "liberal empire" did not take public shape until it appeared in a fall 2003 article by Anatoly Chubais.[10] Chubais had been the architect of Russia's mass privatization program in 1992–93, when I knew him, and then the engineer of Yeltsin's 1996 victory through "loans for shares" from the oligarchs whom privatization had created. But after the economic crisis of 1998 Chubais had made a soft landing as head of Unified Energy Systems, Russia's largest electricity conglomerate. Restructuring began immediately. UES started to pursue debt-for-equity swaps in other post-Soviet countries in 1999. Plans for a "common energy space" in the CIS framework went on the drawing board. In 2000 the North Kazakhstan and Russian grids were reconnected; in 2001 the Russian and Ukrainian grids. By 2003 all Eurasian electricity grids were connected, something never achieved by the Soviet Union.[11] And fossil fuels were not the only factors in play. In November 2002 Putin pledged $2 billion to develop Kyrgyz hydropower as soon as Kyrgyz electricity could reach Russia across Kazakhstan. By the next year the Russian Federation had a strategic economic plan for using energy to advance the state's domestic and foreign policy agenda. And oil and gas were key.

Outsiders remember 2003 as the year Putin arrested Mikhail Khodorkovsky, the ambitious head of the largest, most efficient, and most successful of Russia's new oil companies, Yukos. Like Berezovsky, he too had begun to put money into liberal causes. His arrest inaugurated the grinding down of Yukos through the forced sale of its assets to companies with presidential administration members on their boards. By mid-2005 Putin advisers controlled over $200 billion in key industries; by mid-2006 the figure was heading toward $300 billion; by early 2008, as the Putin-Medvedev switch required some shuffling of boards, their companies were estimated to control some 40 percent of the Russian economy.[12] Khodorkovsky remains in prison in Siberia.

For the outside world his fate symbolizes the creeping renationalization of the Russian economy after the shambles of the transition. When Russians point to how much of it remains in private hands, it is in vain: the world has seen the share of Russia's GDP produced by the private sector drop from 70 percent in 2004 to 65 percent in 2005, and the private share of Russia's oil production drop from 90 percent to 45 percent between 2004 and 2007.[13] The world knows who is in charge of the Russian economy.

As the Putin adviser Igor Shuvalov was to put it with typical bluntness in early 2005, Yukos's fate was intended as a lesson to the rest of those who wished to avoid taxes and prevent the government from fulfilling its social obligations.[14] That lesson hit home: tax collections skyrocketed after Yukos; almost all the oil companies were paying. It almost certainly helped that the international oil price was rising steeply, multiplying revenues for everyone. As the oil price moved toward the $100 a barrel we enjoy today, oil and gas revenues provided higher and higher wedges in have-state GDPs and budgets. By 2006 those revenues accounted for more than half Azerbaijan's

GDP, 30 percent of Kazakhstan's, and (assuming normal market prices) about 20 percent of Russia's. In that year hydrocarbon exports provided over half the revenues in Russia's state budget; for 2007 the expected figure was 52.2 percent.[15]

So there were many straws in the wind, telltale signs of what was coming at home and abroad. Nevertheless, in retrospect 2003 was clearly the breakthrough year for the "liberal empire." By the time Chubais coined the term that fall, his UES had gained control of over half of Armenia's distribution system through debt-for-equity swaps. The conglomerate was "financial manager" of that country's nuclear power plant. It had a controlling interest in Georgia's power grid and a majority share in its power-generating joint venture AES Silk Road. Russia's state gas monopoly Gazprom was dominant in Georgia's energy distribution. In April Russia and Niyazov's Turkmenistan signed an agreement committing two trillion cubic meters of Turkmen gas to Russia through 2028.

I dwell on these moves because they all took place *before* the Rose Revolution in Georgia at the end of 2003. If proof were needed, they show that Russia's use of economic levers to extend its influence was *not* driven by fear of color revolutions or the desire to preempt them. Russia was surprised by the Rose Revolution and reacted clumsily. Using economic levers had just seemed natural. It even seemed "economic."

Putin and other leaders have consistently denied that they are renationalizing the Russian economy, and they have not been insincere. They believe in the market and recognize that it is not just useful but essential. Putin has recognized that Russia cannot achieve rapid economic growth without integration into the world market, that it cannot double its GDP by the target date unless it "creates the proper level of freedom and equal competition"; that Russia must be a democratic and law-based state, and that it will be hard for it to achieve its development goals "under the existing system of administrative control."[16] During the recent presidential transition, new state mega-corporations were being established practically every week, but both Putin and Medvedev also began to hint that once those corporations were on their feet they should dispense with the officials on their boards and shrink back down so as to let the market work.[17]

But just as clearly, Putin has consistently believed that it is up to the Russian state to provide the proper framework for the market, and that the so-called resource sector is key. He has believed it since before he took power in 1999. The Georgetown scholar Harley Balzer has dug up a published synopsis of Putin's 1997 candidate of science degree thesis for the St. Petersburg State Mining Institute, written well before he could have expected exalted office. Its theses as Balzer describes them are consistent with the whole approach of Putin's government to the state and the economy:

> Mr. Putin believes that the state has an important role to play in Russia's economic development process, regulating the resource sector and stimulating the development of large, vertically integrated financial-industrial conglomerates that would be capable of competing effectively with Western multi-national companies. While

relying primarily on market mechanisms to influence development, the Russian government has the responsibility to adumbrate an appropriate mix of market and administrative measures to guarantee development of the extractive and processing industries. These industries could then provide the basis for the entire Russian economy to advance to sustainable development based on high technology.[18]

Hence the new state corporations for aviation construction and shipbuilding too. And when the state-owned Gazprom became the world's third-largest company, Putin noted proudly that it was the Russian state that got it there.[19]

That was where things already stood when Georgia began the cycle of color revolutions, in 2003. At first Georgia seemed an isolated case: it was only when Ukraine had its Orange Revolution, in late 2004, and Kyrgyzstan followed with its Tulip Revolution, in early 2005, that Russians came to see Georgia as having been the start of a cycle. But already beginning in 2003 Russia brought its use of economic muscle to a new level, and its efforts were mainly directed toward its new post-Soviet neighbors. Others were not neglected. Gazprom was interested in Serbia's gas supplies. The Russian government began to promote a second Black Sea gas pipeline to Turkey to parallel the newly opened but underutilized Blue Stream pipeline. It was negotiating with Japan, with China. Nevertheless, Russia's post-2003 activism was most pronounced in the "near abroad," close to home. It sought new partnerships in pipelines, in refineries, in power generation and distribution, in cellular phones. It could be punitive too: in 2005 it forbade imports of meat, fruits, and vegetables from impoverished Moldova; wine was to follow, in 2006.[20]

We should still be wary of the suspicion that goes with the territory in Eurasia, and it is worth noting that in this period the Russian government was careful to justify and explain its new activism in economic or technical terms. Moldova's "frozen conflict," for example, involves its breakaway section north of the Dniester River, in Trans-Dniestria, which has a Russian-speaking majority. Moldova lobbies the international community to reintegrate Trans-Dniestria and tries to press economically in the same direction, for instance through customs controls. When Russia squeezed Moldova in this period, however, Trans-Dniestria was never mentioned; instead, we heard about problems with Moldovan products, about quality control or sanitary standards. The only time Russia strayed from strictly economic ground was when assets were involved that it defined as "strategic," important to the "national interest." Usually these involved natural resources, the focus of Putin's thesis. Occasionally "strategic" was more broadly defined, as when Putin announced that foreign banks should not be allowed to open branches in Russia. In the main, however, these were the years of true "liberal empire": Russian interests were promoted by economic means and justified in economic terms.

The new partnerships did indeed produce new efficiencies—the Armenian and Georgian power sectors worked better and at lower cost to the customer under

UES management—and this also made it difficult to object to them on political grounds.

It is true that by 2005 more and more Russian establishment voices were explicitly calling on the government to use economic leverage for political ends. In July 2005 the State Duma passed a resolution urging the Cabinet to impose new higher prices for gas exported to the Baltic States, Ukraine, Georgia, and Moldova, on the ground that they were trying to join NATO and the European Union. The Duma CIS Affairs Committee chair Andrei Kokoshin urged energy pricing based on the purchaser's foreign policies. Deputy Aleksei Mitrofanov proclaimed, "We should finish with gas socialism!" Still, though Kokoshin was a former deputy defense minister, he was not in government; and the Duma resolution was nonbinding. That same month Putin called for infrastructure to raise gas exports to Europe by forty billion cubic meters by 2010, through a North European gas pipeline on the Baltic floor; but he spoke exclusively in economic terms.[21] Those who saw the Russian imperial hand in every economic connection continued to see it; others were not so sure. By objecting they might have thought they were fighting City Hall. But what if it was just City Market? It was still hard to tell.

2005 On: Liberal Empire No More

In late 2005 Russian actions then changed supposition into certainty: Russia suddenly demanded an exponential increase in the price of gas delivered to Ukraine and when

Ukraine refused, Russia cut off deliveries, in midwinter. A year earlier Russia had intervened in the Ukrainian election on behalf of the Russian-speaking East Ukrainian Viktor Yanukovich, and when his fraudulent election was overturned by the Orange Revolution, Russia was one of the losers too. Now, a year later, Ukrainian politics were gridlocked, with parliamentary elections on the horizon for March 2006. In the uproar that followed Russia's gas cutoff, the conviction of non-Russians that Russia was playing politics with energy became rock solid. With gas disappearing from pipelines in Ukraine, Europe too began to shiver. From Central Asia, Turkmenistan stepped in to help Ukraine with both supplies and prices. In the end a murky compromise was worked out that merely doubled prices (but just for six months) by turning deliveries over to a shadowy Russo-Ukrainian joint venture. Russia was scheduled to chair the next summit of the G-8 industrial countries in St. Petersburg in July, and it wanted to make energy security the agenda centerpiece. But by provoking the year-end crisis with Ukraine, Russia's image morphed for most of the world from that of a partner in energy security to a bully and potential threat.[22]

This was the return of politics to Eurasia's politics, and it came as a shock. The outside world had not really wanted to believe it was dealing with Russian expansionism; neither had many Russians. The Ukraine gas crisis crystallized the world's consciousness that Russia was "back." That stoked Russian pride, but it also made Russia look like an energy muscleman using its muscle for political ends. There was a danger that this perception would poison all of Russia's major issues in world affairs. It threatened bilateral relations with the U.S.—for though the Iraq war had taken the U.S. down a notch, America remained the great validator of Russia's great-power status. It threatened the timetable of Russia's accession to the World Trade Organization, which is after all based on competition rather than bullying by state-controlled monopolies.

So Russia felt prouder, but also more exposed. It responded with a multitrack policy that in an odd way resembled the old Soviet effort to deal simultaneously with governments (correctly) and with revolutionary movements (subversively), and to claim there was no contradiction.

With the West, Russia has been proud to be "back," but has insisted it is there because of its domestic restoration (and of course the good leadership that produced it). "Russia's growing economic potential allows it to play a more significant role in global development," said Putin in 2006. Sounding for all the world like the Soviet foreign minister and president Andrei Gromyko, a spokesman of Putin's went him one better—"It's impossible to tackle vital problems without Russia." Putin's own foreign minister did better still: "In the 1990s . . . some people in the West said they wanted a strong and united Russia. Now we are here. They should be grateful." In 2007, after Putin's very hard-nosed speech in Munich, another spokesman explained that "Russia is back as a major world player," and the Foreign Ministry's annual report judged that "a strong, more self-confident Russia has become an important and integral part of positive changes in the world."[23]

Russia then spent the year showing it was back as a military power too: it tested a new ICBM; it planted a titanium flag at the North Pole; it resumed long-range bomber runs; it sent the fleet back into the Atlantic and the Mediterranean; it threatened to retarget missiles on Poland, the Czech Republic, and Ukraine if they accepted U.S. missile-defense components. The Russian public loved it, and at the end of his tenure as president, Putin was happy to take credit for it.[24]

However, when it comes to using its economic muscle abroad, Russia denies it is being political at all. Russian spokesmen proclaim that Russia is just asking for world market prices for its raw materials. In January 2008, the deputy prime minister and finance minister Alexei Kudrin denied (again) that Russia uses energy as a weapon, saying that market forces are responsible for increases in world energy costs.[25] He could have fooled not just the Ukrainians and Moldovans but now also the Georgians, Belarusians, and Estonians: since 2005 all have been hit by Russian economic constraints, and while Russia invoked technical grounds for all these sanctions, most seem to have followed political steps that Russia dislikes.[26]

Yet Russia also insists on having things both ways. It screams when a smaller neighbor retaliates against its squeezedowns using Russia's own tactics.[27] But the core issue is larger. Russia's tactics on gas to Ukraine mobilized its EU partners to press for Russian ratification of the European Energy Charter it had signed in 1994. Russia has refused on the grounds that ending Gazprom's pipeline monopoly would violate Russia's (legitimate) strategic development vision, and it has worked hard and not unsuccessfully to split the Europeans by making attractive and selective offers; even so, the Europeans have never quite demobilized. After all, as a Lithuanian diplomat in Warsaw put it when Russian "pipeline repairs" shut down crude shipments to his country, "It seems that every step that is taken by a Russian energy company is motivated by politics."[28] And yet we have also seen Putin and others complain of double standards when Gazprom or other firms with heavy government-connected leadership are rejected or deflected from entering Western markets.

There are dual tracks within dual tracks, moreover. Competition over pipelines to carry Caspian Basin energy to market picked up again in 2007 and 2008, but it is now focused on gas. Russia under Putin clearly wishes to make gas the *spiritus movens* of its drive for a new place in the sun, vis-à-vis both its post-Soviet neighbors and the "far abroad" beyond them, using exports through the state-owned pipeline giant Gazprom. This is producing resistance and some pushback. China and India are now in the mix as booming economies facing looming energy deficits; and gas-rich Turkmenistan's mild and ambiguous opening post-Niyazov is whetting appetites all around. In 2008 there were half a dozen new pipeline outlets under negotiation: to Europe from and through Russia but around Poland and Ukraine; to Europe from Central Asia around Russia; to China; to Japan; from Turkmenistan to Pakistan through Afghanistan; from Iran through

Pakistan to India. The age of ownership monopolies may be over (except of course for Gazprom), but competition for dominance via marginal advantage is alive and well.[29]

Meanwhile Gazprom and other state-connected Russian firms bounce back from each rejected suit with redoubled efforts to arrange asset swaps that would build lobbies for Russia in the Western business community, in return for only minority participation by Western firms in Russian exploration and production. For both oil and gas the Russian state has now imposed limits on holdings by foreign-majority firms, excluding them from oil fields above a certain size that are classified "strategic" and squeezing them back down to minority positions at strategic fields where they already had a presence. It wants foreign partners for projects that are remote or otherwise hard to do, and it hopes cash will be enough to bring them in. Oil and gas are not the only sectors affected by renationalization, nor is Russia the only country squeezing: Kazakhstan has been doing the same for oil, Kyrgyzstan for gold. So state consolidation is part of what is going on. But it is also hard to see a state-free market at work.[30]

Russia's remaining oligarchs are proudly private when they venture forth to new conquests in world markets, but foreigners can be forgiven if they see the Russian state looming up behind: for the oligarchs now love their state very, very much. When he donated the cellist Mstislav Rostropovich's art collection to St. Petersburg in 2007, the metals king Alisher Usmanov declared, "Everything I have, I am ready to give to Russia, if it is needed, since I am a citizen of Russia and am proud of it." Oleg

Deripaska was only slightly less lyrical when "he told journalists that he was willing to give his estimated $23 billion fortune to the government at any moment"; six months later the estimate had risen to $40 billion.[31] Just in case, however, the federal tax service announced plans to set up a special unit to audit "major taxpayers" in the fall of 2007, as the election season began.[32] Some of its burgeoning tax revenues went into early repayment of Russian international debt, saving further billions in debt-service, and some went into the Stabilization Fund for social expenditures founded in 2004. By the time it closed, in February 2008, that fund had a value of $156 billion. The main lesson for Russians was the same as for the world: the state was back in charge.[33]

Vis-à-vis the "far abroad," Russia is energized but generally genteel in its dealings. It has struck an arms-for-gas deal with Algeria; an arms-for-oil-products deal with Venezuela; an arms-for-beef deal with Argentina, already a traditional partner for meat. American steel and gasoline distribution, Hungary's airline, Montenegro's aluminum and power, Luxembourg's main oil and gas supplier, gas storage near Berlin, Serbia's largest energy company: the list goes on and on. Nor has it been all one way: Italians, French, Germans, and Americans have bought into Russian firms too. Not all efforts succeed: stabs at Arcelor steel, Alitalia, and Airbus failed for Russians; Renault got the nod to hook up with Russia's largest carmaker, AvtoVAZ, over General Motors (which then moved on to Uzbekistan). Other area countries, especially Kazakhstan, are doing the same or trying to. Muscle helps: cuts in Russian oil supplies to Germany

bring a better deal for LUKoil. Hence the bleats from the EU and the U.S. But even though fewer and fewer believe her, Russia can still claim that sheer economics make these deals work, when they do.[34]

Vis-à-vis its post-Soviet neighborhood, however, Russia has grown increasingly ruthless and increasingly unapologetic as the political subtext has surged to the surface in business dealings. Gas deliveries and prices hold center stage. Prices must be renegotiated at the end of every year, so the end of every year witnesses a high-decibel opera of announcements, leaks, threats, and finally bilateral agreement to what each party will pay in supply costs and transit fees. This annual process is punctuated, however, by mini-crises related to political moves and by new culminations in the massive struggle over new pipelines, which involves a host of outside players, including the U.S.[35] Suppliers virtuously insist they are only seeking world-market prices for their product ("No more gas socialism!"); those supplied accept the argument because they must, but argue on equity grounds for taking the pain by stages, and raise transit prices to compensate where they can. Politically, the only thing lost at every cycle is trust; the only thing gained is the conviction, deeper after every cycle, that for Putin's Russia economics and politics are actually the same.

And by an inversion that only *seems* strange, Russia's insistence that everything is actually economic only makes the problem worse, because it convinces Russians themselves that the world treats them as it does because it is after the resources that have made them great again. As so often, Putin's aide Vladislav Surkov blurted it out best

early on: "People talk to us about democracy, but they're really thinking about our energy resources."

"Some countries," the Foreign Ministry reported in March 2007, "regard Russia as a potentially dangerous competitor on the world economic stage (and seek to restrict) our country's competitive advantages." The next month Putin himself argued that (unnamed) outside forces were meddling in Russia's political and economic affairs in order to "prevent Russia from achieving its own potential." That fall, the Speaker of the State Duma complained that "someone is not happy to see Russia on the world market," but "we won't let anyone intimidate us, either through the WTO or in any other way, because we are Russia." A fortnight later Putin himself was even more pointed, during a three-hour TV Q&A marathon: one of Washington's goals in Iraq was to control the country's oil reserves, he said; Iraq is a small country "hardly capable of protecting itself"; "Russia, thank God, is not Iraq" and *can* protect itself. The next month Putin struck at a statement attributed to the former U.S. secretary of state Madeleine Albright (and denied by her) that Russia has too much natural wealth for one country: "Some people are constantly insisting on the necessity of dividing up our country. . . . They themselves have no wish to share their own riches, and we should take that into account." A month later, he told *Time* interviewers ready to anoint him Person of the Year, "We want to have enough strength to defend our interests and to build good relations with our neighbors and main partners so these partners are interested in seeing Russia develop and grow stronger." Pitching in to elect Medvedev in 2008, he car-

ried on: outside forces had encouraged "separatists" to weaken Russia, but Russia's economy had been growing steadily, so it had returned to the world stage as a strong state. Every Putin statement reflected the same analysis: a global battle for natural resources had begun, he told a nationalist daily in February 2008: "Many conflicts carry a whiff of gas and oil," and this explained why many developed nations were showing increasing interest in Russia.[36] Sad, but genuine.

Russia's effort to dissolve the distinction between economics and politics rings alarm bells for Russia's neighbors and for Westerners as well. It is not simply that melding economics and politics harks back to Soviet times. It is not simply that it makes economic partnerships harder, since behind each Russian partner stands the Russian state with its concentrated economic muscle and willingness to use that muscle for political ends. Alarm bells also ring because Westerners actually believe that separating the economy and the state is a hallmark of modernity as well as an engine of efficiency. To collapse them into each other as Russia has been doing puts a question mark over the capacity of Putin/Medvedev's Russia to join the global economy and the international community. It has raised serious doubt even among the goodwilled about Russia's capacity—whatever its intentions—to *be* modern. And it not only puts politics back at the center of the Eurasian and international agendas with a vengeance; it brings older questions of nationalism and empire in the Eurasian space back to the political surface in a new and more acute form.

IV

STATES, NATIONS, AND
NATIONALISMS IN EURASIA

"And why the sea is boiling hot . . . "

LEWIS CARROLL

If the end of 2005 opened a new era of Russian outward pressure and stiffening resistance from Russia's neighbors, is twenty-first-century Eurasia likely to face rolling turbulence reminiscent of twentieth-century Europe? Part of the answer will depend on whether state-building and state-consolidation in Eurasia will be underpinned by the same kind of ethnocultural nationalism that helped make Europe the last century's "dark continent."[1]

In 2008 it was still too early to say. Russian state actions have told most of the world that Russia has left "liberal empire" behind as its preferred approach to relations with neighbors, and replaced it with something more vigorous, less liberal, and more ominous. There is still no consensus on what that "something" should be called. But since Russia was evidently melding political and economic motives into a single pattern of pressure, its actions have reawakened the old discourse of empire that arose in late-Soviet times and never quite died away in the first post-Soviet years. It has been easy to call what we are seeing just a new chapter in the old history of Russian imperialism.

Yet recent scholarship has made it abundantly clear that Russian primacy in Eurasia has always been hard to compare with more familiar world empires, and if 2005–6 ushered in a new phase of the discourse, the actual situation in Eurasia also contained old and new elements that still make it hard to bring that discourse to a single satisfying conclusion. They indeed revive debate over the fraught old concepts of "empire," "nation," and "state." This is not the place to rehearse the abundant argumentation over how best to define those terms in general and how they apply to Eurasia in particular. That argumentation has enriched our specialized knowledge, and it has provided a firmer foundation for public understanding than we had before. It also fills libraries; just a few of the high points are included in the suggestions for further reading. Let us focus here on two old questions that Eurasia's post-Soviet experience has raised with new acuteness: Can Eurasia produce viable nation-states, and if so, what kinds of nationalism are most likely to fill and drive them?

The historical processes that produced the modern nation-state in Europe were also at work on the Eurasian landmass to Europe's east, the landmass that has come over the centuries to be centered on Russia and Russians. Everywhere, these processes were entangled in subnational and supranational realities, in the politics of kin and class and in the politics of "empire." Nowhere, however, has the intermingling of empire and nation been more confused and confusing than in Eurasia. It has always been almost excessively difficult to fit Russia into any other pattern of empire: her geography and her experience are just too different.

Whereas most other great empires extended a metropole's power overseas, the tsarist empire arose as a patrimonial state in constant external conflict with the decaying overland empires against whom it was built. Over its centuries of existence it made a series of efforts to define itself by simplifying itself. It drew sometimes on indigenous concepts, and sometimes on imports from abroad—usually from Europe during in the eighteenth and nineteenth centuries. These included monarchism, religion, versions of "Russianness," even a version of "Eurasianism." None of these concepts achieved primacy. The quandaries were even expressed in language: Russian makes a distinction that exists in no other tongue, between *russkii,* ethnic Russian and usually Orthodox, and *rossiiskii,* of the Russian polity; and that distinction is very old.

Russia simply contained too many peoples with too many different historical experiences and trajectories to be understood in simple categories. Their consciousness of themselves began with the family, rose (sometimes) to the level of "people from here," then to distinct ethnic and language groupings, all overlaid by an autocracy demanding and negotiating support from a ethnically syncretic nobility.

These groups-in-consciousness were all somehow kin based, but they were also often associated with religion.

In some cases, as noted earlier for the North Caucasus, struggles for hearth and home against encroaching Russians became more religious—in that case Islamic—as they fought on, as a way to unite normally warring tribes and clans against outsiders. Conversely, Russians tended to categorize those they were trying to subdue by religion rather than ethnicity. The Russian Imperial Census of 1897 asked respondents about their religion but not about their nationality.

Thus denied, by the early twentieth century nationality became the Empire's time bomb, as nationalism; if it exploded only in some places, it was ticking everywhere. Super-aware of the danger, the Bolsheviks who took over in 1917 were also supercreative: the ethnofederalism they built into the USSR when they established it in 1923 generated nations in order to destroy nationalism. By the second half of the century the Soviet Union contained a cluster of republics with full-scale state institutions but no genuine political autonomy—none of the self-determination their constitutions proclaimed.

The Bolsheviks reversed the tsarist order when it came to categories. Soviet censuses had no question on religion (and there is none in Russia today); they asked only about ethnicity and language. Every individual was identified by ethnic "nationality" through the famous Paragraph 5 on the internal passport introduced under Stalin. The effect was to create ethnocultural communities to which everyone belonged. But although republic and autonomous regions had titular ethnic majorities and names, these communities were peculiarly virtual, since they were not in fact tied to territory. Millions of people lived outside their titular republic, including twenty-five million Russians. Inside "their" Russian Republic, conversely, about a sixth of the population came from elsewhere in the Soviet Union.

That kind of ethnocultural nationality was (quite intentionally) not much of a building block for nationalism. Neither, as it turned out, was language.

It is true that language became more and more important as the Soviet experience drew on, in consciousness and in policy. Both policy and practice made the Russian language hegemonic across the eleven time zones of this huge state with its integrated economy. As I noted earlier, its hegemony also increased with time—assimilation was in fact beginning to work in the years after Nikita Khrushchev—and the resistance it met from fearful new elites sometimes took "national" form.[2] The late-Soviet struggles between regions and the center were not just struggles over resources.

Yet it was hard to be an anti-Russian nationalist because the Russians themselves presented such a diffuse target. They were at ease with their superiorities, but those superiorities were also subconscious (often) and underinstitutionalized (always). The tsarist empire that the Soviet Union succeeded had been built and ruled in the name of God, and the Soviets ruled in the name of the universal classless society of the future. Indeed, the British scholar Geoffrey Hosking has argued that until 1991 Russians never actually had a nation to feel part of or look to.[3] During my time in Moscow in the Brezhnevian 1970s, the joke was that since all the tsars had German blood, and Stalin was a Georgian, and Khrushchev was a

Ukrainian, Leonid Brezhnev was the first Russian to head Russia since Boris Godunov, at the dawn of the seventeenth century. It was a joke, of course: Khrushchev was actually a Russian from Ukraine. But even those who feel Hoskings goes too far can perhaps agree with the political scientist and historian Ronald Suny when he writes: "My argument is not that Russia did not succeed in building a state, but that she succeeded too well in building an empire and failed to create a 'Russian nation' within that empire."[4]

Like the other Soviet republics, the Russian Soviet Federative Socialist Republic (or RSFSR) was entirely a creation of the Soviet Union, but it had even fewer separate institutions than they did. Even as a Party-state Russia was hollow by comparison, since unlike the others it had no separate Communist Party. Russians might be at home and at ease with their identity, but that identity was often *Soviet,* because it was Soviet state citizenship that ensured it. The Party line, moreover, proclaimed that nationality was legitimate but nationalism was doomed, and it was often easiest just to believe it. In Soviet conditions there was no room for any real growth of alternative ideologies—Eurasian, Pan-Slav, Orthodox—either.

The Soviet Union's collapse took everyone by surprise. Non-Russians and Russians alike now had to create new "claims and visions."[5] All had to build states in a new world where resources were declining fast and steeply and then fill those states with new national identities.

I tried to show earlier how sovereignty and resource issues wove in and out of politics in the first post-Soviet decade. Western countries—which were both victors in the Cold War and partners in the post–Cold War world —promoted liberal internationalism, civic rather than ethnic definitions of citizenship, good neighborliness, and peaceful negotiation in place of violence. This prescription had some genuine appeal. It set the standard of modernity that most post-Soviet leaderships wanted for their country, and it defined the international community they wanted to join. Hence it served as a counterweight to the rabid ethnic nationalism that also sprang up in the ruins of the USSR. Vicious national hatred appeared not only in the new republics but also in Russia, reaching backward to the Black Hundreds of a century before and sideways to the skinheads next door in post-Communist Europe.

That ethnic nationalism was authentic, and it left its footprint on a score of places. The question was whether it could gain political ascendancy and last. Where people were threatened by war, around Russia's borders, in Moldova, in the Crimea, in Nagorno-Karabakh, politics were indeed ethnicized. In Tajikistan conflict sparked around region and affiliation, with one side hoisting the banner of Islam. In Estonia and Latvia conflict sparked on language and memory: both religion and language could easily be taken to define ethnicity. The twenty-five million or so Russians living outside the new Russia were transformed overnight from first among equal subjects in the Soviet state to subjects of states dominated by non-Russians; it was a shock. Within a few years eight million of them left for Russia, where by 2000 4.3 million had stayed. Armenia and Azerbaijan also traded populations. More recently the pace has slowed, as conflicts stay

frozen and economies pick up, to what is in fact unusu-
ally low territorial mobility of populations. Migration is
now mostly for jobs, mostly temporary, mostly to Russia.[6]

But in the early years after the fall it looked as if an
unmixing of peoples was under way, and Yugoslavia
showed how bloody such a process could become. Governments across the region struggled to come up with
policies to deal with it. Russians tried to assert a special
status for themselves in the near abroad, Russia's new
post-Soviet neighborhood. They promoted dual citizenship; they plumped for Russian as an "official language"
alongside the new non-Russian "state languages." These
uncertainties and responses prolonged the discourse of
empire of the late Soviet period, to be sure, but did so in
a new way, for now Russians themselves were involved.
In the USSR they could still afford to be comfortable, be-
mused, in denial; now many felt almost helpless, sometimes desperate.

Certainly these new dilemmas and fears helped generate some of the sovereignty claims that swept the region
and sparked wars in the borderlands and years of separatist unrest in the Russian Federation itself. Suddenly
rank-and-file citizens and local elites together were demanding defense, demanding rights, demanding resources, declaring "sovereignty"; and often these demands
were justified on an ethnic basis. I have described how
these played out in Tatarstan, but the same phenomenon
emerged in a score of other places. And of course in
Chechnya it spiraled downward into war and butchery.

But when it came to dealing with these urgent new

problems, Russia at least had its inherited Soviet state institutions, plus some new ones. Many were deteriorating
and unsuited to the new national tasks that Russia's now
partly privatized economy and diminished place in the
world were creating. But at least they existed; they could
be used and adapted. For the new republics it was much
harder. They too inherited Soviet institutions, but those
had not been designed for independent governance in the
first place, and they were also more rudimentary. So the
challenge of the new post-Soviet world was greater for
Russia's new neighbors. Ukraine and Belarus had had
seats in the United Nations and foreign ministries and
missions in New York to service them, but Moscow had
called the shots. And while Russians could at least reach
back to pre-Soviet or even Soviet national discourse—
among Slavophiles and Westernizers, Eurasianists, Pan-
Slavists, "indigenizers"—most of the new governing
elites could not, and had to start almost from scratch.[7]
History was ransacked for foundation myths: Tamerlane
with his mountains of skulls for Uzbeks, a "Sanjar tomb"
in Merv—ascribed to a medieval monarch but perhaps
not a tomb at all—for the Turkmen, a medieval physician
for Tajiks. For the non-Russian peoples of Russia, finally,
it was even worse: their state institutions were weakest of
all, their "national" discourse almost nonexistent.

Socialism had collapsed with the Soviet Union, and
while it lingered on in a political half-life in some countries including Russia, it was no longer politically competitive. Many in those early years expected religion to
rush into the void left by socialism—the more so since

"values politics" were getting stronger in the democratic world as well.

To some extent religion served as expected. The Russian Orthodox Church gained strength in Russia and among Russians in Central Asia. In Ukraine three Christian denominations were in vigorous competition with each other and with mainly Protestant evangelicals. Islam revived in Central Asia and to a lesser extent in the Caucasus and among Muslim populations along Russia's Volga. Churches, schools, and mosques multiplied across religion's bare landscape.[8]

Yet for the first post-Soviet generation religion has proved itself incapable of substituting fully for defeated Communism. Taken *sub specie aeternitatis* fifteen-plus years is not long; religion may yet fill the spiritual void Communism left behind. But it has not yet done so, and there are several reasons why.

First, the religious revival has been led by denominations that were tainted by their subordination to the Soviet state, and that taint has only deepened with the efforts of all the successor states to assert control of religious leaderships. Fear of the Taliban before 2001 and fear of an al-Qaeda brand of radicalism thereafter made Islamic leaders special targets for state tutelage. Tajikistan's civil war between post-Communists and Islamists was brought to an end in 1997 because the Taliban's 1996 takeover next door in Afghanistan had so frightened their Russian and Iranian sponsors. But all these new states inherited a desire to control religion from their Soviet past, and they all found reason to keep in practice.

Second, it has simply been hard to define a stable role

for religion when there is so much ethnic and religious mixture. Russians are "born" Orthodox, and Putin has actively patronized the Russian Orthodox Church; he stood proudly by in May 2007 when its two branches reunited after eighty years of separation.[9] But if there were twenty-five million mainly Orthodox Russians living outside Russia, there were also fourteen to twenty million Muslims inside Russia, and as Putin himself put it in June 2006, "They're not immigrants. They are full citizens, and this is their native land."[10] Defining citizenship in religious terms was all too likely to create disaffection and encourage disloyalty, which every state in the area was eager to avoid.

Third, the onslaught of evangelical Protestantism that began after Soviet prohibitions dropped away and has never abated threatened all the established denominations, provoking a circling of wagons that discouraged infighting among them. In Kazakhstan, for instance, Orthodox and Muslims came together in an "alliance of natural religions." But this common fear of evangelical dynamism made it harder for their leaderships to promote ethnoreligious nationalism. It has led them back to the door of the state, whence so many of them had started in the first place.[11]

The upshot has been that post-Soviet religious leaderships have devoted most of their time and energy to cultivating relationships with state authorities, rather than to saving and winning souls. Spreading piety seems less urgent than knitting and maintaining connections with power. The dwindling Jewish communities in Russia and Ukraine look to outside supporters as well as to the

Russian and Ukrainian states, but this just means they look doubly dependent.[12] In other words, instead of boldly competing for ideological primacy in the new post-Soviet world, religious elites operate much like anyone else: they struggle for access to resources through competition for marginal advantage focused on the state and its elite factions.

The first corollary has been that religion has become more and more a badge of ethnic identity, but within the old Soviet paradigm of ethnocultural "nationality" rather than in terms of more modern ethnic "nationalism." The situation is dynamic. Tatarstan celebrates its Muslim roots with a "restored" mosque that may not have existed previously. The small group of Turkic Chuvash people west of Kazan are looking back to pre-Christian roots to validate their nationality. The even smaller number of Mishar Tatars, who live among the Chuvash, stress their medieval Islamic origins. In both cases, however, the origins must be practically invented and exemplified in "reconstructed" mosques and "restored" cemeteries. In Kazakhstan there is even an effort to invent a whole new religion, called Tengrism, as the "natural religion of the Turks." Meanwhile, however, one estimate puts actual church attendance among the Orthodox at 7 percent; in one survey only 3 percent of Jews believe that practicing Judaism has anything to do with being a Jew. One is born to a religion, but identity has little or nothing to do with religious belief or observance.[13]

The second corollary is that in this part of the world at least, the future of nationality has almost everything to do with state power.

Much the same is true of that other classic attribute of national identity (and classic apple of discord in nationalist discourse): language. In the Soviet Union national or titular languages were cultivated as elements of nationality without nationalism, and there was some retribution in the 1980s. The Estonian and Latvian revolutions, for instance, were spearheaded by language, millions of people singing the old songs in a crucible of new national identity. "Language laws" emerged all over the area, even in the Soviet Union itself just before the end, in 1990; the new Russia ground slowly toward a new law that stressed minority languages less, Russian as a "state language" more.[14]

In half a dozen countries titular languages were now proclaimed "official languages" ahead of Russian; Kyrgyzstan's government has resisted pressure to give that status to Uzbek.[15] Once Latvia and Estonia became independent their leaderships tried to make titular language capability a criterion for state citizenship, with mixed results. In Tatarstan within Russia, in Kyrgyzstan and Kazakhstan outside, language laws provided for compulsory education designed to increase public use of titular languages that were spoken mainly at home. Uzbekistan, Turkmenistan, and finally Kazakhstan embarked on long marches toward the Latin alphabet (or a version of it in Turkmenistan's case) for their titular languages.[16]

At the extreme, Turkmenbashi's Turkmenistan shut down any school teaching in Russian, English, Uzbek, or Kazakh; Moldova's Russian-majority Trans-Dniestria shut down its Romanian-language schools in 2004.[17] Russians also pushed back elsewhere, to make Russian a "regional" and then an "official" language in Ukraine, and an "official language" in Kyrgyzstan. The late-Soviet and post-Soviet language scene has been nothing if not lively.

The struggles go on. But in 2008 it appears more and more that the outcomes have to do mostly with the consolidation of state sovereignty. Where language is a contentious issue it usually means the state is in political trouble; where states are growing more stable and accepted, so is the titular language, even by minorities, and the language issue itself fades from political prominence.

At one extreme, in Belarus, where national consciousness is fluid and the dictatorial state promotes confederal union with Russia, the government has shut down Belarusian-language schools and held a referendum that makes Russian the second official language; installing a Belarusian-language version of President Lukashenka's website is scarcely compensation. In between, the tussle over Kyrgyz and Russian continued in postrevolutionary Kyrgyzstan: late in 2007 President Kurmanbek Bakiyev was still promising enforcement of the state-language law to strengthen Kyrgyz instruction in rural schools, while also stressing the importance of learning Russian. Language laws in Kyrgyzstan, Kazakhstan, and Russia's Tatarstan do appear to have raised public use of the titular languages, but they have done little to change home use, which continues to favor Russian. At the official level there was even some backsliding to Russian-language teaching: after all, Russian had become the language of power once more.[18]

But just as power does not flow just one way in today's

Eurasia, so too with language: Russians outside Russia are accommodating to the languages of the new states ruled by others in which they now live.[19] Ukraine is the most striking example. Out of power the East Ukraine Russian-speakers' party may bang away for a referendum that would make Russian an official language. Beneath the surface, however, poll results show that while Russian-speakers are indeed increasingly conscious of their language, they are just as consistent in their support of independent Ukrainian statehood, and more and more likely to send their children to Ukrainian-language schools. And we see the same trend into titular language schools among Russian minorities in Latvia and Estonia. That, after all, is the most plausible path to jobs and power, once a decent future in the new state seems plausible too.[20]

It is possible to discern a trend in Eurasia toward ethnocultural nationalism under state sponsorship, with thorny old questions of defining citizenship to be worked out and new ones arising. That would be the classic "European" model of nation-state development, the one that gave us two World Wars and post-Yugoslav breakdown. It implies a degree of ethnic unmixing, forced or unforced, and a degree of homogenization, spontaneous or, more usually, under state auspices. The vector sums of migration, demographic, and language trends in Eurasia point rather inconclusively in that direction. In mid-2006 the Russian government announced a three-year program for "repatriating" three hundred thousand Russians from outside Russia's new borders. There were also economic and demographic motives at work—declining

birthrates and out-migration affect Siberia especially—
and there is certainly nasty ethnic nationalism around,
among Russians as among other Eurasians. Hate crimes
have multiplied, usually directed against people of color.
Non-Russian stallholders have been a special target, and
the government has colluded by banning non-Russian
citizens from retail trade. The repatriation program is
also ethnic unmixing by state policy. So some ingredients
of the "classic" nation-state of unblessed memory—ethnic nationalism and state sponsorship—are there.[21]

But both ingredients are likely to be sharply limited by
other realities. Low levels of ethnonational consciousness
are maintained partly by state power: Lukashenka's government *chose* to shut down Belarusian-language schools.
Ethnic mixtures will continue to be widespread: Russians
and Ukrainians and Kazakhs in Kazakhstan, Ukrainians
and Russians in Ukraine, Moldovans and Russians in
Moldova, not to speak of the Baltic republics. The repatriation program is yielding a trickle rather than a flood
—four hundred people, thirty-five thousand inquiries
the first year—and it turns out the Russian state wants to
lure back not only Russians but some of the two million
Germans who fled west after 1991; that is, economics tops
ethnicity.[22] Some Russian ethnic nationalism and some
Russian state sponsorship will be there. They will produce friction, tension, some nationalist backlash elsewhere in Eurasia. In the absence of catastrophe, however,
ethnic cleansing—genuine and final homogenization of
a national territory—is not an option. The minorities are
too large, the world has changed too much. States can no
more confess to the goal of ethnic purity today than they

can confess to imperialism. These are the rules in the world that post-Soviet countries want very much to join.

The desire to join the West was critical in lifting the new Baltic republics up from their initial impulse to discriminate against and extrude their Russian minorities, up onto a "European" level of civic citizenship. But civic citizenship, a civic rather than ethnic definition of national identity, is almost forced on all the new states by the sheer size of the minorities, the sheer degree of mixing, and, last not least, the common Soviet heritage of portable ethnocultural identity independent of territory. All the factors—these ground realities—militate against the use of state power to favor titulars, and encourage the use of state power to protect minorities even where protection is not institutionalized. All limit legal discrimination and favor the institutionalization of toleration.[23]

These factors affect Russia too. Russians have been living with *russkii* and *rossiiskii,* with Slavophiles and Westernizers, for a long time now. In the post-Soviet era more and more Russians think about what it means to be a Russian, but they still find there are no easy answers. Language issues are one test: when calls to secure or promote Russian are heard in Crimea or elsewhere in Ukraine, it is a sign of political tension. But the uncertainties also show up in debates over "a possible emerging national ideology," as the Kremlin deputy administration head Vladislav Surkov put it (rather delicately) in 2006.[24]

There are various candidates for the role. "Eurasianism" is one. It is actually a nexus of ideological strands, with many internal contradictions—like the region it purports to describe and actually constructs—but all wrap around a central conceptual thread, the idea that the landmass of which Russia and Russians are the center has produced a unique civilization, neither "Europe" nor "Asia" but finer than either—more humane but still powerful—at least potentially. In one sense Eurasianism is as old as the backlash to Peter the Great's Westernizing reform, or as Russia's nineteenth-century Slavophiles. But in place of the individuals and classes to which twentieth-century Westerners looked for explanation, Eurasianists see "civilizations" or "cultures" as the personae of history, primordial actors created by geography and genetics. In that sense, Eurasianism is as new as any of our other contemporary fundamentalisms. It also changes shape and point depending on the user. For most of its history, it justified Russian rule over Eurasia's other peoples. Today it has resonance with both Russians and their neighbors, but for different reasons. It is strangely popular in Central Asia, especially in Kazakhstan, as a rationale for the ties with Russia and other post-Soviet states its governments promote. By contrast, Eurasianism tells Russians that the catastrophes of the twentieth century— both Communism and the chaotic 1990s that followed— are insignificant compared with their "natural" destiny to be first among equals from the Baltic to the Bering Strait, in the teeth of alleged American opposition. It is mainly an intellectual movement; its acolytes seek the ear of the great, rather than power for themselves. But in Eurasian universities and among the great it has some resonance, and bears watching.[25]

To a lesser degree the same is true for "sovereign democracy," put forward by Putin supporters like Surkov to capture Russia's new sense of pride and defend it against foreigners who criticize its departures from democracy and constraints on civil society. It says that democracy is whatever Russians choose it to be, free of "dictates" from outsiders. It might be called a post-Soviet version of the Brezhnev-era "really existing socialism," which also sought to defend shabby reality against carping criticism.

Neither of these candidates has really caught on as a new national ideology. Surkov's "sovereign democracy" was disavowed first by the majority pro-government party, Unified Russia, then by Dmitry Medvedev when he was deputy premier, and finally by Putin himself. Medvedev's problem was that "any time one attaches a qualifier to the word democracy, it gives the impression that what is meant is something less than full-fledged democracy," and he has repeated this support for democracy without adjectives in his run-up to the presidency. Putin did not elaborate; in fact, he mused to his audience of Western Russia–watchers that discussion of "sovereign democracy" is "useful." Sure enough, some months later the State University in provincial Chelyabinsk established a "Center for Constitutional-Legal Studies of the Problem of Sovereign Democracy." "Why should all disputes be settled in the European Court [of Human Rights]" the Chelyabinsk law dean asked indignantly, "when half our country isn't in Europe but in Asia? We need to create, say, a Eurasian Humanitarian Court. Why shouldn't we create a unified moral-political space with our neighboring former republics?"[26]

Eurasianism may have a longer life, since it has deeper

roots in Russia's intellectual past and is also linked to the Russian urge to delve deeper into the old neighborhood. But a careful study of Eurasianism in action by the Thai scholar Paradorn Rangsimaporn shows that the concept as used by Russians today has no religious or ethical content of any kind: it is entirely geopolitical, entirely about the Russian state in the world.[27] When Surkov had the wind in his sails he was convinced, RIA Novosti reported, "that his concept of sovereign democracy, in which Russia defines what its democracy is and accepts no criticism from abroad, 'appeals to the dignity of the Russian people and the Russian nation. It's about who we are.'"[28] Now that the concept is dead in the political water, its lack of content lives on.

When Putin touts the values that Russians share with Europeans, he mentions "respect for international law, rejection of force to settle international problems, and preference for strengthening common approaches": all governing the practice of *interstate* relations. Indeed, Russian leaders glory in precisely this "pragmatism," this lack of ideology, this occupation of space vacated by the Americans. Within it, though, there is little in the way of values, as distinguished from practice, that might be worth imposing or that others might wish to share. The Russians are not the only ones: when violence erupted again in Georgia in late 2007, it was partly because the victors in the Rose Revolution had put their emphasis on "restoring territorial integrity and strengthening the Georgian state, rather than on continuing democratic reforms." (The fact that Georgia has no values to offer its breakaway regions may help explain why it has proved so hard to restore Georgia's territorial integrity.) But the emptiness within is perhaps starkest in Russia, as some Russians recognize: "I call this the 'model of instrumental democracy'—not values-oriented, not philosophical, not ideological, not political, but very, as they say now, user-oriented."[29] And that is the main point: the void left by Communism in today's Russia is being filled—at least up to now—by an ideology that is almost always defined exclusively in terms of the restored Russian state's great-power status.

In the current post-Soviet moment Russia shares much with its new ex-Soviet neighbors. Not every single one is focused on building state institutions. Since its civil war ended in 1997 the dominant faction in Tajikistan's power-sharing government has built power rather than institutions; in Kyrgyzstan factions are more balanced, so power is spread around more, but institutionalization also suffers.[30] Today, however, most Eurasian states are bent on building themselves.[31]

Sometimes they try to build themselves by working together, as evidenced by the alphabet soup of new regional organizations that have sprung up, mainly under Russian sponsorship, since 1991: CIS, CSTO, EURASEC, SES, and the rest. When they have not been entirely ineffective, they have been modestly useful precisely where they are needed to support national state-building—delimitation of borders, extradition, and citizenship rights and responsibilities. State-building goes forward on a bilateral basis too, both within Eurasia and with Western partners. My favorite result has been the creation of a Kazakhstan Navy on the Caspian, but this is one among many: border controls are being strengthened—borders *created*—almost everywhere.[32]

All these states, moreover, continue to ransack History's cupboard for new ideological or emotional content with which to fill their new borders. Kazakhstan in particular was galvanized by the gross insults in Sacha Baron Cohen's film *Borat* into a major campaign of cultural self-creation; the gorgeous historical drama *Mongol* was one of five Oscar nominees for best foreign-language film in 2008, but that is only the most visible result. Building culture out to national identity has been a major program in Uzbekistan as well. In fact almost everyone is doing it; and they are finding as they keep on that the cupboard is not so bare.[33]

Hybrids will appear, some perhaps staying forever. Hybrid sovereignty is a feature of the international system—think of Hong Kong, Guantánamo, more recently Northern Ireland, Bosnia, Kosova—and there is no reason not to expect it in Eurasia. Soviet legacies and Soviet mixtures will continue to mark not only hearts and minds but institutions and interstate relations. Often "empire" issues piggyback on them, as a result of ambiguities that look more and more anomalous just because Westphalian sovereignty is more and more often the aspiration, the goal. For now, though, hybrids are all over the Eurasian landscape, and will be for a long time to come.

Some are as simple as border-crossing regimes, often informal, to ease the lives of citizens who used to travel freely in areas where there were no borders "to speak of": in Central Asia's Ferghana Valley, for instance, now divided among three independent states; between Moldova and its Trans-Dniestria; among the enclaves that dot both Central Asia and the Caucasus. There are also ingenious arrangements of what has been dubbed "exchange sovereignty" to deal with what were once Soviet commonalities: Russia's Black Sea Fleet in Ukraine's Crimea, or Russia's Baikonur Cosmodrome in Kazakhstan.[34]

But there is a brand of hybridity that is more ominous because while it can point toward the past, like exchange sovereignty or dual nationality, it can also point toward a nastier future, and it is hard to tell which sort of hybrid any given case will turn out to be. One example of the latter sort are the privileges one state grants to citizens of another state, with the implication of an extension of sovereignty across the new borders. Russia does most of the granting: fifty thousand Kyrgyz with Russian passports in 2006, seventy thousand in 2007; sixty-five thousand Russian-speakers in Moldova's Trans-Dniestria eligible to vote in Russia's December 2007 parliamentary election; Russian passport holders in Georgia's restive Abkhaz and South Ossetian regions giving Putin's United Russia 86 and 92 percent of their votes respectively.[35] But the Russians were not alone: Moldova complained bitterly that Romania was giving passports to perhaps eight hundred thousand (or 38 percent) of Moldova's 3.4 million citizens, and Belarus bridled at a raft of privileges for its ethnic Poles passed by the Polish parliament in September 2007.[36] It is not un-European—in the 1990s Romanian-Hungarian relations were hamstrung for years over Hungarian privileges for Romania's Magyar-speakers—but it could be Europe of the worst kind: ethnocultural nationalism sponsored by the state. In Russia's case, though, the privileges went not just to Russians outside Russia but to clients who were not Russian, that is, they expressed a state interest without ethnic content. So it is important to judge carefully whether a given grant is nasty encroachment or benefaction, or both.

That ambiguity points us toward another distinction that is important for assessing Eurasia's future in the world. Across Eurasia, including Russia, and despite the hybridities, the overall drift is toward the crisper, more Westphalian sovereignty many of these new national leaderships want for their countries and themselves. Most of the work and most of the progress has been on building not a new federation, nor a new confederation, nor varieties of mixed sovereignty, but on building individual nation-states with exclusive sovereignty over defined territories and governments with exclusive legitimate control over the instrumentalities of violence.

And it may in fact turn out that Russia's neighbors are more capable of evolving into that kind of "classic" nation-state than Russia is itself. It may be around Russia's borders rather than within Russia itself that ethnic nationalism with a cultural or religious basis provides the ideological or ideational content for the emerging consolidated state.[37]

Other distinctions will also be at work. Even aside from Russia, Eurasia's new states are not just similar but also all different, and the differences are pronounced when it comes to the nation-state prospect. Clan-based politics or pronounced ethnic mixing can inhibit it in some countries. In others those two factors can drive development toward a civic or cultural patriotism like those in the American or French traditions. Such processes could well be under way in Ukraine or in Kazakhstan. Many permutations are possible. But for the whole post-Soviet space the nation-state prospect will appeal, and in most of that space it is the most plausible potential political format for development that is available today.

Where the nation-state format takes hold, it can generate conflict between the resurgent Russian state and the emerging nation-states in the Eurasian backyard. But such conflict is not the only option. There will also be variety in Russia's relations with its new neighbors. None face territorial absorption: old-fashioned imperialism's day is done. Friction between Russia and Georgia's Rose Revolution legatees has been endemic and has produced no pearls, but Georgia has reabsorbed one of its defecting regions, Adzharia, and Russia has withdrawn from its military bases in Georgia. Russian leaders from Putin down have repeatedly disavowed territorial ambitions, and they are probably sincere, if only because border changes are so threatening to Russia itself. Even if Belarus and Russia succeed in negotiating some kind of "union," it will fall short of conflation. Subordination is another matter. Some elites in some countries—Belarus, but also Armenia—will be drawn to degrees of cooperation with Russia—for economic advantage, for protection against others they fear more, or simply in response to Russian pressure—that can put them on a slippery slope toward subservience.[38]

As we have seen, though, Russia is not the only Eurasian state in the process of consolidation: so are all the rest. There are degrees of strength and weakness, coherence and confusion. But over a decade and a half of post-Soviet experience, all without exception have become more "like" states, in their institutions, in their habits, in their capacities to define and pursue policies and to defend themselves. They have become states in ways they never were before. As such, they resist rather than seek subservience to other states, and they are better able to do so with each passing year.[39]

All of Russia's neighbors are weaker than Russia, so they will look more to the outside world for support in defending themselves against Russian pressure, Russian encroachment, Russian blandishments. But at present Russians are even less likely than their neighbors to define their national "claims and visions" in terms of ethnic or cultural superiorities and inferiorities. Like their neighbors but more so than their neighbors, they will look to the outside world for validation and self-definition. For the present—and probably for a long time to come—Russians will define their destiny in terms of the fortunes of the Russian state in the world.

This means in turn that the Russia the world will be dealing with in these next years will not be a Westphalian nation-state that is buoyed forward in both offense and defense by a cohesive ethnocultural nationalism. As I have noted with regard to hate crimes, that kind of nationalism exists in Russia, is ugly, and can turn violent. But most Russians, including those running the Russian state, do not have that particular twentieth-century fire in their bellies. That much is spared us so far. And as long as that is true we need not fear a repetition on Eurasian soil of twentieth-century Europe's large-scale rolling hatreds.

Russia as well as its neighbors will be attentive to the rules of state conduct and fitness standards in the international community that are defined by the twenty-first-century international community itself. Russia's boisterous return to the world stage may be a point of pride for Russians, but if it is to be successfully sustained it brings with it obligations too.[10] With oil at $100 a barrel, Russia may not care much about foreign investment (although if its industry is to remain productive it will begin to need technology that only foreign investment can bring, and state-dominated Russian firms have had defeats as well as victories in their search for foreign partnerships). But even if it is indifferent in practice to investment, Russia will still seek "the bubble reputation," and in our day and age it is to be found less "in the cannon's mouth" than in respect for human and minority rights, in civic citizenship, in democratic freedoms and pluralism.

Pressure to pursue these virtues may indeed come more from outside than from inside Russia. If the twentieth-century nation-state brought internecine mayhem to Europe, it also brought modern democracy, and until Russian governance is democratic in spirit as well as in form, Russia will probably not be much of a force for either democracy or mayhem. But the thirst for a good reputation nonetheless gives international standards real impact, and the outside world will have leverage on Russia far beyond investment needs; by pushing back and holding to those standards, the rest of the world can put its own inflections on Russia's "claims and visions" for itself.

The good international reputation these states hanker for is also less easy to come by than it was in the heyday of Westphalian sovereignty. If Westphalian sovereignty still prevailed in pure form, the Russian state's position in the world would be independent of Russia's internal political or economic situation. However, that principle has been tarnished by the twentieth century's nationalist excesses, and also by late progress in formulating universal norms of behavior that include formerly "domestic" arrangements once sealed off by exclusive sovereignty from international concern and scrutiny. And in practice, as I have shown, Russia's domestic political situation and capacity to exert influence abroad both depend crucially on its position in the international economy.

So the Russian state's new assertiveness in the world will have both economic and political facets. Ordinarily the world would bridle if this renewed outward pressure were overtly political but wink if it remained economic, as under Russia's "liberal empire" formula. But where ambiguity and uncertainty had reigned before, in the Ukrainian gas price crisis of December 2005 the Russian state gave the world a new vision of Russian "imperialism." The effect was probably unintentional: certainly the East-West debate over energy security that has dragged on ever since has featured one long litany of Russian hurt feelings, self-justifications, misunderstood good intentions. But it created new facts and a new situation: whatever its intentions, Russia convinced the world that it intended to push out and onto its neighbors for political ends using economic means.

Russia's conduct since then has on balance merely perpetuated the conviction that it is all muscle and no heart. But just because so much depends on consciousness in today's world, today's Russia also has an option to erode or reverse that conviction by changing its own behavior—handsome is as handsome does. As in so many ways, Russia's current behavior takes us back to Gorbachev's time. It recalls his effort to relieve the world's pressure on a faltering Soviet Union by doing what it took in practice to break down the world's "enemy image" of the USSR. Usually, sovereign states prefer to be obdurate, like Putin's Russia so far: it is certainly not faltering, so its hybrid successor may also prefer to plough ahead down the path marked out by Russia's just rights and perfectly legitimate intentions. It is sometimes forgotten that Gorbachev in fact succeeded in eliminating the Soviet Union's enemy image abroad; what Russians today remember, in any event, is the collapse he ushered in at home. They are therefore unlikely to find the precedent appealing: truculence and obduracy are more in keeping with the present mood. So at least in the short term Russia has produced a challenge to itself, to the world, and to the United States.

V

TODAY'S EURASIA AND THE UNITED STATES

"And whether pigs have wings."

LEWIS CARROLL

What does this Eurasia mean for the United States, and what should the U.S. policy approach be?

As a global power the U.S. will always be interested in Eurasia and engaged with its peoples and nations. Eurasia is too large and important a part of the world to be ignored. It casts a shadow of the old Soviet threat forward in time, and its axis—the Russian Federation—is nuclear armed. So are its neighbors: China to the east and India and Pakistan to the south; and there are others in the queue. Eurasia's new nations are players on today's most urgent global issues: terrorism; counterproliferation of weapons of mass destruction (WMDs); economic stability and growth (including its energy centerpiece); stable political development (including democratization, its long-term key). U.S.-Russia relations are now too small a piece to capture all that is important to us about Eurasia. Even Eurasia as a whole is too small for its weight in the world to be self-evident; a policy focus that brings back the old Cold War triad that included Europe as the queen of East-West battles would not restore Eurasia to its former bulk on our policy landscape. China and India to Eurasia's east and south are fast joining Europe as global powers, with sustained economic buoyancy superior to Europe's and military muscle approaching hers and perhaps more usable. So the context for why Eurasia matters is very large. Eurasia itself is not what it used to be as a factor defining U.S. interests and policies, but there is not much disagreement in U.S. politics as to its high and continuing importance.

The U.S. has had a modest shaping role in Eurasian developments since the Soviet Union dissolved: as a beacon of hope, as a partner, as a lightning rod for area discontents. In general, though, U.S. policy toward the post-Soviet space has followed those developments at some distance, with some lag. That is partly explicable in terms of U.S. ideals, and even more in terms of traditional U.S. practice in foreign affairs. For both are forward leaning.

Thus, U.S. policy was fairly realistic about Eurasian realities in the early 1990s, about how hard it would be for Eurasians to achieve democracy, the market, and good-neighbor relations with outsiders old and new. But it wanted to help them toward those goals and it wanted to believe they could be reached. So it tended to gild the lily. Similarly, U.S. policy was fairly realistic in the late 1990s, as the limits to forward progress were being reached, as economic reform slowed and authoritarian regimes spread across Eurasia. But it wanted to believe that the original goals were still valid, that we still shared basic modern values with Eurasian governments. So it tended to see regressions as bumps in a road that was still there, and to respond slowly.

Inertia is appropriate to a wealthy great power: after all, as Edmund Burke taught us, "Property is sluggish, inert, and timid."[1] But U.S. inertia in the face of Eurasian developments exposed U.S. policy to nagging criticism for being too soft on "Putin's Russia" once Putin's Russia shifted into gear in 2003. Academics came first, true to their role as stormy petrels, already by the end of 2003, the year of Khodorkovsky's arrest.[2] Establishment opinion makers followed in 2005 at the beginning of President George W. Bush's second term.[3] Thereafter the cry was taken up by major politicians, both in the Democratic opposition and in the president's own party, by Senator John McCain.

Yet it turned out that the administration had the luxury of responding slowly—in a statement by then secretary of state Colin Powell already in 2003, statements by Condoleezza Rice as Powell's successor beginning in 2005, in the State Department's annual Country Reports on Human Rights—because the issues were complex (and thus hard to understand), and because by the time the political critics came together—in statements by Senators McCain and Joseph Lieberman and by Congressmen Tom Lantos and David Dreier in the run-up to the St. Petersburg G-8 summit in the summer of 2006—they were overshadowed by more dangerous and pressing issues such as Iraq and Lebanon.

And over the years since then, the administration has

continued to be fairly successful in rebalancing its policies toward Eurasia in response to trends in the area. It has had knowledgeable and capable people in charge, and the fact that Eurasia has not been on the policy front burner has also helped. The chronic time lag between area developments and U.S. responses also drains credibility from Russian charges that the U.S. is now a neo-Bolshevik power driven by a mad democratization ideology intended to destabilize the post-Soviet space. To the extent that ideology has been a factor in the U.S. approach to Eurasia, it has in fact encouraged inertia: the U.S. government has wanted to believe in the aftermath of 9/11 that we could still be "strategic partners" with Putin's Russia, as proclaimed in 2002 , because it wanted to believe we still share values with Russia even though Russia was showing a hard nose to the world and insisting that its domestic affairs were off-limits in principle. As the new realities sank in, however, a new consensus has slowly emerged in U.S. policy and opinion that supports a new and fairly adequate mix of policy views and directions. It is a consensus that has taken and survived some fairly stiff shots from the new Moscow.

This consensus holds that Eurasia is important for global strategic stability and economic security and that Russia is an important partner for the U.S. on key global issues: for the war on terrorism; for WMD counterproliferation (including nuclear weapons security and specific issues like Iran and North Korea); for stable development of the global economy (including energy security and Russian WTO entry). It holds that we are not competing with Russia for primacy in the Eurasian space: there is no new Great Game. At the same time—the consensus also holds—for U.S.-Russian partnership to be sustained even on a limited range of issues where we share interests, we will also have to share some values. Hence, and for that reason, we will continue to express concern at Russian government pressure on democracy, on civil society, on Russia's neighbors. We will do so in private but also in public. And we will keep supporting civil society and the independence and viability of Russia's neighbors, where we can, just because such support is called for by values we deem universal, and just because we need something in common with Russia in order to pursue common interests together.

Over recent years the U.S.-Russia time horizon has looked on occasion like a Himalaya range of erupting volcanoes. At a meeting with ex-Soviet and ex-satellite presidents in Vilnius in May 2006, Vice President Richard Cheney trumped the Council on Foreign Relations Task Force and blistered Russia for restricting rights at home, bullying its neighbors, and using energy as a political weapon. Nine months later Putin used a speech in Munich to accuse the U.S. of "almost uncontained hyper use of force" which he said was undermining global stability; and, he added, "it has nothing to do with democracy, of course." The newly inducted defense secretary Robert Gates gave a mild response, but Senator John McCain was also in the audience and was prompt to hit back: "Will Russia's autocratic turn become more pronounced, its foreign policy more opposed to the principles of the Western democracies and its energy policy used as a tool of intimidation?" Two months later, Putin's VE Day speech had a passage comparing U.S. policy to Hitler's.[4]

The U.S. response at lower levels was muted but unrelenting. Speaking in Berlin the week after Putin's Hitler analogy, U.S. assistant secretary of state Daniel Fried called for sustained engagement mixed with firmness to try to "help" Russia during its "unfinished transformation." "We do not want a weak Russia, but a strong Russia must be strong in twenty-first-century, not nineteenth-century terms. . . . A strong center is part of this healthy mix. But a strong center in a state of weak institutions is not." And "[We] should not pay a price for cooperation, nor indulge Russia when it behaves as if a residual sphere of influence over its neighbors is its due." In late May, his deputy, David Kramer, was more pointed still. Then, a week later, President Bush kicked off an eight-day tour of Europe by complaining that reform in Russia was off the rails, "with troubling implications for democratic development," and he once again celebrated freedom: "The most powerful weapon in the struggle against extremism is not bullets or bombs—it is the universal appeal of freedom. . . . Freedom is the design of our maker, and the longing of every soul."[5]

Since then the rhetoric has cooled somewhat, in the leadership encounters in Maine and on the Baltic Coast and in other high-level statements. But neither side has given ground on the substance of their disaffection. At the World Economic Forum at Davos in February 2008, Secretary Rice dismissed talk of a new Cold War as "hyperbolic nonsense," but she also called on Russia to work toward a "transparent and open global energy economy" and argued that "Russia's greatness will ultimately be secured best through greater political freedom for its people—and through the establishment of strong institutions that check the power of the state, rather than serve the interests of a few."[6] Lecturing is just what the new Russia and its leaders hate most.

But while the gods were trading punches on the heights, in the valleys below the shepherds were tending the sheep, the little flock of interests that could be common to the U.S., Russia, and its new neighbors. The larger animals—counterterrorism, nuclear nonproliferation, the Middle East peace process, some kind of arrangement for energy security—are fairly familiar; but the flock of interests included other issues too.

Helpful sheepdogs were part of this valley landscape. They included scholars who were perturbed at the disintegration of comity, and who continued to point to the layer of common interests just below the discordant surface, and to suggest creative ways of showing the world that layer was there.[7] But the sheepdogs also included officials who kept saying how important it was to keep steady where we can and should.[8] It is hard to parse just which forces matter when, but the upshot has been that America's "complicated relationships" with Russia and the rest of Eurasia have somehow lumbered forward through some hard years.

Part of the tale has been tonal: all sides have lowered the decibel level and softened the rhetoric. Partly, though, it has been substantive. The relationships are broad enough to include positives as well as negatives, and both have required their share of tending. To be sure, sanctions have not dropped out of the tool kit, but lying alongside them is a whole range of transactions and interactions, many in the counterproliferation and counterterrorism fields, that look ordinary yet are anything but.[9]

There has even been room for real creativity. It has not touched all thorny issues: for example, U.S. policy on independence for Kosova appears to have been all consistency all the time. But creativity was at work when it came to dealing with the other hot-button dispute of 2007, U.S. plans to install missile-defense components in Poland and the Czech Republic. Again, it is hard to analyze any given step in depth: in these matters "open covenants secretly arrived at" is often the ticket. But creativity there has been. The best-known instance has been Putin's proposal that the U.S. comanage an existing Russian radar in Azerbaijan and forgo its East European radar deployment. But the U.S. has had its share too, hard to follow but unmistakable, in the form of proposals to broaden the context and modulate the pace of missile-defense deployments. And if the press has given Putin the credit, that has been okay too.[10]

With presidential transitions looming in both capitals, each has had an incentive to set their bilateral relationship on an even keel that will guide it through to the next phase, and this combination of consistency and creativity has allowed them to do so. They began to think about it fairly early on, in fact. After the "Lobster Summit" in Kennebunkport in July 2007, Putin's aide Sergei Prikhodko told reporters that the presidents had concluded enough had been done to ensure the preservation of what is positive in U.S.-Russian relations after they leave office; "There is certainty about this on both sides." Still, it took another nine months for them to give concrete form to what had "been done": it came in March 2008 with a Bush letter carried by Rice and Gates to Putin in Moscow, involving a "joint strategic framework document," a kind of road map for negotiations on issues that could probably be agreed on by the end of 2008. Counterterrorism, nuclear nonproliferation, and trade were mentioned, a list capacious enough to include both Iran's nuclear potential and U.S. missile defenses in Eastern Europe. And such a framework could well keep the agenda of U.S.-Russian common interests stable until a new U.S. administration took charge in 2009. Who the U.S. interlocutor would be at that point was of course unknown, but Dmitry Medvedev was there for his first postelection encounter with Americans and announced that "Russia" was "determined to go ahead."[11]

Nor are relations with Russia the only arena where steadiness and flexibility combined have produced results for the U.S. Central Asia has a life of its own that extends far beyond U.S.-Russian relations, but the competition of outsiders for influence there has been a major part of that life, especially since 9/11 and most especially since the color revolutions of 2003–5. The Tulip Revolution in Kyrgyzstan in March 2005 was followed by a political explosion in Uzbekistan's eastern city of Andizhan in May; repression followed; Europe and the U.S. lined up to reprove the repression; Russia and China lined up to support it. And in July the Shanghai Cooperation Organization (SCO), with Russia and China nodding gravely, gave the U.S. base in Uzbekistan the back of its hand: the U.S. was out by November.

Repression and reproval combined thereafter to make Uzbekistan a world pariah. Yet the three years since 2005 have witnessed a slow comeback, comparable with the calming and consolidation in U.S.-Russian relations. Here too, no one backs off on the principles. The U.S. keeps saying democracy and the market are Uzbekistan's better future; Uzbekistan keeps telling the U.S. to butt out. But here too it proves possible to figure out ways to move forward. Two years after the SCO "invited" a U.S. timetable for withdrawal from the Uzbekistan base, the remaining U.S. base in Kyrgyzstan was somehow not mentioned at the SCO summit in that country's capital. Later in 2007 a new U.S. ambassador in Tashkent met with the country's human rights ombudsperson, the daughter of its long-time Soviet-era Party boss. Early in 2008 President Karimov received the U.S. Central Command head Admiral William Fallon for a cozy "exchange of views on subjects of mutual interest." And not long after, it turned out, U.S. troops, along with those of all other NATO countries, would have access to the Uzbek base at Termez on the Afghan border.[12]

Such successful combinations of a lot of consistency and a little guile have secured the U.S. administration enough political support to sustain the policy of "cooperate where we can, push back where we must"; to keep it going through its tenure; and to pass it on to its successor. There is and will be criticism, for being too tough, for not being tough enough; but that too is traditional for U.S. policy toward Eurasia. Such policy may not take the U.S. a long way, but it can go on for a long time.

The question is whether that kind of policy will really equip the U.S. to deal effectively—to promote and defend U.S. interests in timely fashion and at acceptable cost—with the Eurasia described in this book. I suspect it will not, because it still tries to deal piecemeal with too many features of the Eurasian scene. To become truly effective, U.S. policy needs a sharper focus on fewer factors.

There may not be many other choices. Time and disappointment have already drained away whatever overoptimism U.S. policy once brought to dealing with post-Soviet Eurasia. Nor will it ever revive: never again will we imagine that we can cause or prevent decisive developments in Eurasia as we would in a world closer to our hearts' desire. Among scholars, the contained indignation of the 2006 Council on Foreign Relations study— titled "Russia's Wrong Direction"—had given way by late 2007 to the kind of weary resignation that permeates a fresh run-through of the issues for the Center for Strategic and International Studies, more chastely titled "Alternative Futures."[13]

It is a mood that affects government as well, and not unnaturally after so many years in the saddle. In 2008 Americans realize that we work within limited margins. We recognize that Eurasia will always be competing for attention and resources with other, usually more pressing issues. We know that its countries will be players on boards where we play too, but usually not the central players. We will approach them with limited fears; we already approach them with limited expectations.

Within a framework thus defined by realistic modesty, the U.S. will nevertheless still grapple with Eurasia's least plausible but most dangerous prospect: a grim and dour stability punctuated by explosions in individual countries, a future of rolling turbulence that saps them all. That is probably not the future; but as a prospect it has a genuine reality, and if it became the future it would be highly damaging to U.S. interests, regardless of which player or players prevailed. The U.S. would inevitably be called in to defend the weak against the strong, and would be damned if it did and damned if it did not.[14]

It is important at this point to define "weak," because in today's Eurasia *every country sees itself as weak*. Even the strong feel they are barely escaping from weakness, and justify bullying their neighbors by their own recent debility. U.S. policy will therefore have to make its own judgments on strength and weakness.

To be "strong" a Eurasian country will have to have or hope to have state institutions that are dominant in the national economy and that can be used to enhance that country's position in the world. By that criterion Eurasia's "strong" countries are Russia, Kazakhstan, Azerbaijan, and Turkmenistan. All have fragilities and dependencies. But whether they feel weak too should also not be the issue for the U.S. when it is solicited to intervene in situations of mounting intra-Eurasian tension. At that point it should simply not listen when bullies cry "weakness" and use it to justify their bullying.

Some of those neighbors will be genuinely weak. Some

Eurasian countries will be vulnerable to outside pressure because they lack essential resources, economic or political, and they will be even more prone to vicious factionalism in politics as a result. Each situation is specific, but such weakness helped push Tajikistan and Moldova toward civil war in the early post-Soviet years. It helped push three other countries—Georgia, Ukraine, and Kyrgyzstan—toward their color revolutions. It may well be that those civil wars and revolutions opened up a positive future in ways that would have been unthinkable in Soviet times. In today's post-Soviet present, however, they solved little. All five countries continue to struggle with huge problems toward uncertain destinies. Their convulsions have left them with looser, more flexible politics that allow each to defend its interests better (eventually even in Georgia), so that each can avoid the worst consequences of weakness. But the new tensions and new openness bring new temptation to call in outside help: in Georgia from the U.S. and NATO, in Ukraine from NATO and the European Union, in Kyrgyzstan from almost anywhere.

Russia has a resurgent state that is consolidating its control over the economy and society in the name of state nationalism. Russia will be an important partner for the U.S. on a whole range of global issues, and it will be important to the U.S. that Russia be a responsible partner. Here Russian state nationalism can be an asset, since it tends to immunize Russian leaders from the kinds of ethnocultural nationalism that dominated early twentieth-century Europe at such disastrous cost.

Today's Russia can be compared in some ways to Wilhelminian Germany. It too is a new state in old territory with somewhat incoherent institutions, striving perpetually from a late start for a place in the sun of world power. It is a state that bullies its neighbors, and it is a state that defines its status first of all in terms of prestige. That kind of state can be unpleasant, nasty, even in some specific cases a bit dangerous for other members of the global community. And this new Russian state's neighbors are all the more vulnerable because relations are no longer constrained by the Soviet ideology, which demanded (and promised) fraternal cohabitation under a single sovereignty forever.

Yet this Russian state is also without most of the overheated ethnic and racial nationalist content that made twentieth-century Europe so turbulent and so bloody. And it is likely to fill up with such content only in conditions of prolonged turbulence across the twenty-first-century Eurasia of which it is so central a part. At the time I write, that kind of Eurasian turbulence seems unlikely, but it is made more likely by the fact that Russia's small new neighbors are indeed more susceptible to ethnic and racialist nationalism than Russia is. Some are already at war—even if Eurasia's conflicts are now merely "frozen." All are politically tempted to appeal to the U.S. to save them from Russian domination.

The U.S. will in turn be tempted to try. Just as Russians are no longer constrained by the USSR (except in their heads), neither are Americans. Intervening on behalf of Eurasia's weak is in the finest Wilsonian tradition. The impulse will be tempered by prudence, by the pull of competing priorities, by the course of events on the ground, as it has been in the case of Chechnya. But it can rekindle, and there will always be good reasons to carry the torch of freedom forward. Americans usually believe that domination of others is destabilizing at home and abroad. They do believe that on the scale of the planet only a community of market democracies can be truly stable.

Both propositions may even be "true" in the long run, true as these things go. In the short run, however, what the post-Soviet space needs most is a stable development of state institutions within which democratic politics can grow, because these institutions provide stable space for factional political struggle in which contestants have more and more interest over time in playing by commonly accepted rules with broader and broader participation. Such state institutions were Communism's secret gift to Central and Eastern Europe (compared with the rickety state structures of the prewar period), and then only in degrees that differ by country. They could be Soviet Communism's secret gift to the post-Soviet states of Eurasia. Ukraine, Tajikistan, Kyrgyzstan, even Uzbekistan are not precisely strong states, but even they compare well with the ramshackle tsarist state before the Soviets. To become that secret gift, however, state institutions must be nurtured.

The U.S. is already doing some of the right things. Its assistance programs in the Eurasian area include help for institutional development, help for political development, help for market reform, programs that encourage respect for human rights and fundamental freedoms. Its diplomacy—private and public—targets the same priorities

where it can. But if the U.S. or indeed any outside partner is to maximize the democratic prospect in situations
like Eurasia's, where civil society is weak but where ethnic and racialist nationalism is still also weak, they need
to focus much more clearly and consistently on today's
elites and the national state structures on which those
elites overwhelmingly depend.

Rather than on tomorrow's civil societies, in other words,
the focus of U.S. policy and resources in Eurasia should
be on today's states. They will be the incubators and mid-
wives of tomorrow's civil societies, and without them the
latter are unlikely to emerge at all.

It is also worth noting that a U.S. policy focus on today's Eurasian states would be within an honorable U.S.
foreign policy tradition. In what turned out to be the late
Cold War, from the late 1960s to the late 1980s, U.S. policy toward the Communist world certainly encouraged
and supported dissent and emerging civil society. But the
bulk of U.S. policy and resources focused consistently on
Communist *governments* and the elites that operated
within their ambits. Partly this was because Communist
governments gave us few alternatives, but it was also a
matter of calculation, of strategy. On our side, the people
we sent on exchanges and leader grants were free men
and women, but the people who came to the U.S. on such
programs had official connections, and were likely to return to work in official capacities. The U.S. government
wanted to expose Communist-country elites to Western
ways, to help them develop Western connections, to join
what at one point was called a "web of vested interests" in
improved and peaceful relations (on both sides) that

would make a nuclear world more stable and safer. The real targets, in other words, were Communist governments: along with macropolitical and macroeconomic leverage, we saw people-to-people contacts as leverage to encourage governments—over time and at the margins—to cooperate and to liberalize.

Once again, Eurasia today is not the Soviet Union; it is not even neo-Soviet. It follows that U.S. policy should not be neocontainment. It is in our interest and in keeping with our ideals to help Russia's neighbors be independent and viable states. But the aim should not be simply to wall off an authoritarian Russian state and wait for its implosion. Because of advances in technology since the Cold War, Russia could not seal itself off if it wanted to, and the outside world could not seal off Russia if it wanted to. Moreover, the rest of the world has no interest in doing so: on the contrary, it is by welcoming Russia as one of its own that the world community can best help make Russia a responsible twenty-first-century partner.

For Russia's dependence on the outside world for its very self-definition gives the outside world more leverage on Russian state policies than it ever had on the Soviet state. Even in its late stages, when it was setting aside proletarian revolution in favor of "all-human values" or "a common European home" as the lodestars of its foreign relations, the Soviet state was still very largely self-defining. Today, nearly two decades after the Soviet Union dissolved, Russia's state-nationalism-without-content makes the rest of the world the arbiter of Russian national identity.

Russia's neighbors are of course also now part of the "rest of the world" for Russia, even though many Russians would still prefer it otherwise. State-to-state relationships within Eurasia vary, and some will be important building blocks for Russia's emerging self-image, for good or ill. Weak neighbors will be tempting targets for Russian state nationalism, spuriously legitimated for Russians by geography and Soviet legacies. Strong neighbors will provide lessons in good twenty-first-century international behavior. And how the far abroad approaches intra-Eurasian friction will help determine the Russian approach to the wider world as well. Acquiescence in Russian bullying will be seen by many Russians as "good," and "realistic"; assistance in pushing back will be seen as "intervention," as "interference," as "double standards," as a "new Cold War." But as state structures strengthen in both Russia and its neighbors and as new balances are established, passions will cool; until then, Russian hurt feelings are predictable and traditional. They will not make the critical difference on most policy issues.

What will be critical instead will be the articulation of Russian state interests in the far abroad—Russia's status as a power in world affairs. That status will also be defined by practice rather than ideological content. But the practical issues that determine it will represent a much broader range of common interests with other powers than will issues between Russia and its post-Soviet neighbors. The Russian state under Putin already recognized that broad range of interests. The hybrid regime that is following it in Moscow can be expected to proceed along the same path. It should be encouraged to do so by U.S. government policy practice, and applauded when it does.

Individual issues are of course crosscutting in their ef-

fect on policy because they are important to different political constituencies. The problem of linkage—how to
relate Russian interest in certain issues to U.S. interest in
other issues—will always be there. How Russia treats its
neighbors will affect the capacity of the U.S. to cooperate
with Russia on larger issues, just as that capacity is affected by how Russia treats its own citizens. The reason
is the same in both cases: Americans have come to believe
that over the long term, aggressive, bullying behavior by
a powerful state at home or vis-à-vis its neighbors will
translate into contempt for U.S. interests too.

These are traditional dilemmas, however. The U.S.
government was obliged to deal with them in relations
with the Soviet Union, and it managed to do so effectively. It can do so even more effectively now because its
leverage, as an important element in Russia's international environment, has in fact grown since Soviet times.
It has grown not because Russia has weakened (although
it is weaker by many power criteria) but because Russia's
reputation in the world is more central to what Russia's
elites want their country to be—a respected, esteemed
world power—than it was even to Soviet leaderships.

Here the U.S. is in a privileged position. The American Enterprise Institute scholar Leon Aron's assessment
of 2006 remains accurate today:

> Perhaps the key American resource, the most desirable
> thing the United States can give Russia is esteem and
> equality. No matter how much America is castigated in
> the pro-Kremlin or Kremlin-owned newspapers or tele-
> vision channels, no matter what is being said about

"Asia" or "Eurasia" as new national destinations, today, as under Lenin, Stalin, Khrushchev, Brezhnev, Gorbachev and Yeltsin, for people as well as the elite, a parity with America—be it in strategic nuclear missiles or corn, meat or steel, democracy or coal, outer space or Olympic medals—and its appreciation of Russia has always been a key legitimizing domestic political factor. When it comes to Russia's national self-respect, no one else—neither Europe, nor Asia, nor yet Germany, China, France, or Japan—even comes close.[15]

Yet the U.S. is not alone; others do count too, and increasingly so. In seeking to make twenty-first-century international standards of conduct the acid test for Russia's good name in the world community, the U.S. will find many allies. Some will be emerging great powers like India and China. The first among them will be the oldest—the old-new European Union—because its members, new *and* old, are in practice the front line of the struggle to work out peaceful and respectful habits in international relations for both Russia and its key neighbors to the west.

But potential members of a "coalition for a responsible Russian great power" will include Russia's new neighbors themselves, and here there is an additional fringe benefit. If it is true that Russia's small neighbors are actually more prone to ethnoreligious or ethnocultural nationalism than Russia itself, it is also true that the best way to tame that kind of nationalism and encourage its civic alternative is to give these new states the realistic prospect of joining international institutions that incorporate and demand twenty-first-century standards of conduct. In the postwar period NATO membership was fragile south-eastern Europe's best solvent for ethnic nationalism of just that kind; NATO and the EU might fulfill the same function further east in the years ahead. That is surely the lesson of the struggles over language and citizenship in the Baltic republics since independence; it can apply else-where too.

The U.S. has properly taken the lead in making NATO and EU membership a live prospect in the post-Soviet space. But by spreading its priorities so thin it has brought upon itself some nasty backlash from sitting regimes. Since the color revolutions became a series and a concept, the democratization element included in the NATO/EU prospect is associated with regime change, with a Western intent to overthrow the governments in place. If the prospect of "joining the West" is to be an ef-fective engine for conduct in accordance with twenty-first-century standards, it needs to be drained, not of its democratization element, but of grounds for suspicion that its true intent is subversive. Suspicion will always be there: this is a paranoid part of the world, and for good experiential reasons. But right Western policy can also squeeze that paranoia down below the level where it trig-gers repression at home and truculence abroad. The proof, again, is from the late 1980s, when U.S. and West-ern policies toward Gorbachev's USSR were strong in defense of Western values, but included so much engage-ment with the Soviet state that it was impossible to blame "the U.S./the West" for Soviet weaknesses.

Today as well, the key for effective U.S. policy will be

to step back toward a more traditional focus on states as our government's primary counterparts and partners in world affairs.

In some others parts of the world, technological advances may have eroded the classic nineteenth-century nation-state into something milder and more open. Elsewhere, they may have smudged interstate borders. Elsewhere, they may have made states less critical as factors in world affairs. That could be the case for Western Europe or for North America or for Japan. In still other parts of the world the classic nation-state may still be beyond reach. That could be the case in parts of Sub-Saharan Africa. In Eurasia, however, the state is very much the name of the game.

In the post-Soviet space the nation-state is not a relic of the past but the wave of the future. Among all the alternatives on offer in the international system, ranging from tribalism to universalist utopias, in Eurasia the nation-state is and will remain for many years to come the most plausible and effective vehicle for ensuring identity, welfare, and even prosperity through effective governance. It will not be the pristine Westphalian nation-state of yore; it will be partial and marbled through with interdependencies. At the fringes there may well be mixed sovereignties galore. But it will still be closer to the nation-state we in the West may be leaving behind than to the merely formal segments of an essentially borderless global community that dreamers have projected for mankind since the eighteenth century, and always in vain.

The question is not whether the Eurasian nation-state will emerge but what sort of content it will have. It will be the character of its animating nationalisms that will determine what sorts of partnerships and what sorts of competition the U.S. will face in Eurasia over the next decades. If all or most Eurasian nationalisms are ethnoreligious or ethnocultural on the old West European model, of the kind most natural to Russia's new neighbors, Eurasia will be an area of mounting interstate tension in which states clamor for the U.S. to take sides, and in which taking any side damages larger U.S. interests. If most Eurasian nationalism becomes state or civic nationalism reminiscent of the American or French varieties, in which citizenship is defined in terms of choice and equal rights—of the kind most natural to Russia—it will still be possible to resolve Eurasian tensions through negotiation within an increasingly robust framework of rules and standards shared among Eurasian states and with the outside world.

The U.S. has limited influence in Eurasia, and Eurasia is only one region in a world where many vital U.S. interests are transnational or global in character. One U.S. interest in that world, however, is to use our limited influence to encourage the consolidation of civic nationalism—and the containment of ethnic nationalism—among Eurasia's emerging nation-states. To do so, we need to deal with them primarily *as* states.

We need to deal with them "as if" they were responsible and capable participants in an international society with twenty-first-century standards, to be sure. But—if we are serious about fostering the right kind of nationalism—we cannot have it both ways, as the Soviets and other ideological regimes are inclined to try to do. It may be possible elsewhere, but in Eurasia, for the reasons set out in this book, the U.S. cannot act as both a state and a revolutionary movement. Because of their weakness and the weakness of the civil societies they bear in embryo, today's Eurasian states cannot be dealt with effectively "as if" they were mere shells of or enemies of tomorrow's possibly more attractive civil societies. If we try to deal with them that way, we shrink the chances that such civil societies will emerge, and inflate the chances that these states will monopolize public life across Eurasia in our still-new twenty-first century and that they will be driven in their relations with the outside world by the kind of nationalism that nearly crippled Europe forever in the twentieth.

We can do better than that in Eurasia. But if we are to treat them as responsible states and demand that they act like responsible states, we need to act like a responsible state ourselves. In fact we usually have, in this past half century, even when we preferred to see ourselves as the City on the Hill, with citizens in charge who intended to return to the plough. To resolve that contradiction we will need to embrace a paradox: we do best as a City on the Hill when we see ourselves first of all as a responsible state in world affairs and act like one. We can do it; if we are to have an effective policy for the long term in post-Soviet Eurasia, we owe it to ourselves to do it; and both our major parties are fully capable of doing it. We can, in the spirit of bipartisanship, recall one of Ronald Reagan's little jokes and apply it in developing a solid state-based policy for Eurasia, even though the joke was about voting Republican: It only hurts the first time.

NOTES

Introduction: Getting Beyond Eurasia's DNA

1. Victor Erofeyev, "Russia's Last Hope," *New York Times,* February 29, 2008.

2. To borrow language from Mark R. Beissinger, "The Persisting Ambiguity of Empire," *Post-Soviet Affairs* 11, no. 2 (April–June 1995): 149–183.

3. Thom Shanker, "Administration Rebukes Putin on His Policies," *New York Times,* June 1, 2007. The official is David Kramer; I once had a version of his job.

4. Jonas Bernstein, "While Saying Centralized Power Is in 'Russian DNA,'" *Radio Free Europe/Radio Liberty Newsline,* October 18, 2007, http://www.rferl.org [hereafter RFE/RL].

I. The Weakness of Civil Society

1. Theda Skocpol, *Diminished Democracy: From Membership to Management in American Civic Life* (Norman: University of Oklahoma Press, 2003).

2. See Robert D. Crews, *For Prophet and Tsar: Islam and Empire in Russia and Central Asia* (Cambridge, MA: Harvard University Press, 2006).

3. Terry Dean Martin, *The Affirmative Action Empire: Nations and Nationalism in the Soviet Union* (Ithaca, NY: Cornell University Press, 2006).

4. See Dmitry P. Gorenburg, "Soviet Nationalities Policy and As-similation," in *Rebounding Identities: the Politics of Identity in Russia and Ukraine,* ed. Dominique Arel and Blair A. Ruble (Baltimore: Johns Hopkins University Press, 2006), 273–303, esp. 297–300.

5. See Grzegorz Ekiert, *Rebellious Civil Society: Popular Protest and Democratic Consolidation in Poland, 1989–1993* (Ann Arbor: University of Michigan Press, 1999).

6. M. Steven Fish, *Democracy from Scratch: Opposition and Regime in the New Russian Revolution* (Princeton, NJ: Princeton University Press, 1995), 61–74.

7. The penalties for dabbling in politics spiked after the color revolutions of 2003–5 and have remained high, see e.g. Liz Fuller, "Armenian NGO Head Downplays Funding Cut" (after he had joined the political opposition), in RFE/RL, August 29, 2006, and Patrick Moore, "Russia Shuts Down EU University," RFE/RL, February 12, 2008: "Academics at the EUSP said the move . . . followed a row last year over a program funded by the European Commission to improve the monitoring of Russian elections."

8. Between 1993 and 1995 I was Coordinator of U.S. Bilateral Assistance to the New Independent States of the former Soviet Union, based in the State Department, and I write from personal experience on these aid priorities and issues.

9. Kelly M. McMann has been the bard of this aspect; see her essay "The Civic Realm in Kyrgyzstan: Soviet Economic Legacies and Activists' Expectations," in *The Transformation of Central Asia: States and Societies from Soviet Rule to Independence,* ed. Pauline Jones-Luong (Ithaca, NY: Cornell University Press, 2004), 213–245, and subsequently "The Shrinking of the Welfare State: Central Asians' Assessments of Soviet and Post-Soviet Governance," in *Everyday Life in Central Asia: Past and Present,* ed. Jeff Sahadeo and Russell Zanca (Bloomington: Indiana University Press, 2007), 233–247.

10. The vivacity of government affiliated organizations can be seen in Robert Coalson, "Nashi Forms Group for Children as Young as 8 . . . and Continues to Patrol Moscow to Prevent Orange Revolution," RFE/RL, December 7, 2007; and, later: Coalson, "No Longer Needed, Nashi Is Scaled Back"—"There is no longer a threat of an 'Orange Revolution,'" RFE/RL, January 29, 2008; and Coalson, "Nashi Commissars Deny Reports of Group's Demise"—"The group could become an opposition party if it feels that United Russia is not paying enough attention to the policies of Vladimir Putin"— RFE/RL, February 4, 2008.

11. On civil society structures, including the GONGO, and their interrelations with one of Eurasia's toughest states, see Alisher Ilkhamov, "The Thorny Path of Civil Society in Uzbekistan," *Central Asian Survey*

24, 3 (September 2005): 297–317; and some idea of civil society's range outside Russia can be had from Babken Babajanian, Sabine Freizer, and Daniel Stevens, "Introduction: Civil Society in Central Asia and the Caucasus," *Central Asian Survey* 4, 3 (September 2005): 209–224.

12. See Kathryn Stoner-Weiss, *Resisting the State: Reform and Retrenchment in Post-Soviet Russia* (Cambridge: Cambridge University Press, 2006) and Richard Giragosian, "Reputed Armenian Crime Figure Gunned Down," RFE/RL, August 10, 2006.

13. Roger Sapsford and Pamela Abbott, "Trust, Confidence and Social Environment in Post-Communist Societies," *Communist and Post-Communist Studies* 39 (2006): 59–71; Timur Dadabaev, "Public Confidence, Trust and Participation in Post-Soviet Central Asia," *Central Asia-Caucasus Analyst* (May 31, 2006), http://www.cacianalyst.org.

14. Human Rights Watch, *Choking on Bureaucracy: State Curbs on Independent Civil Society Activism,* HRW Report Index no. D2001 (February 20, 2008), http://hrw.org/reports/2008/russia0208/.

15. Robert Coalson, "Government Awards Presidential Grants to NGOs," RFE/RL, November 8, 2007. For the overall context, see Michael McFaul and Kathryn Stoner-Weiss, "The Myth of the Authoritarian Model: How Putin's Crackdown Holds Russia Back," *Foreign Affairs* 87, 1 (January–February 2008): 69–84.

16. Patrick Moore, "New Pipeline Route to Steer Clear of Lake Baikal," RFE/RL, May 26, 2006, with citations to earlier reports.

17. Soul-searching and criticism of misguided aid programs went hand in hand, and had already turned into a groundswell in 2002–3: see a whole issue of the journal *Demokratizatsiya* 10, 2 (Spring 2002), with a worried introduction by Michael A. McFaul, 109–16; also see Sarah E. Mendelson and John K. Glenn, eds., *The Power and Limits of NGOs: A Critical Look at Building Democracy in Eastern Europe and Eurasia* (New York: Columbia University Press, 2002); then Marc Morjé Howard, *The Weakness of Civil Society in Post-Communist Europe* (Cambridge: Cambridge University Press, 2003) and Sarah L. Henderson, *Building Democracy in Contemporary Russia: Western Support for Grassroots Organizations* (Ithaca, NY: Cornell University Press, 2003). Probably writing as Putin took over in Russia, these scholars were the canaries in his mine shaft; but the salutary chirping has continued.

18. "[Putin] still has this desire to look like a civilized Russian modernizer," the political observer Lilia Shevtsova said in December 2007, quoted in Clifford J. Levy, "Russia's Knockoff Democracy," *New York Times,* December 16, 2007.

19. Andrei Illarionov, "Russia Inc.," *New York Times,* February 4, 2006.

20. Valerie Bunce and Sharon Wolchik, "International Diffusion and

Postcommunist Electoral Revolutions," *Communist and Post-Communist Studies* 39, 3 (September 2006): 283–304.

21. Liz Fuller, "Armenian Presidential Ballot Follows Georgian Scenario," RFE/RL, February 21, 2008.

22. "[The] country appears to have moved, at least temporarily, from a context of 'democracy without democrats' to one of 'democrats without democracy.'" Lawrence Broers, "After the 'Revolution': Civil Society and the Challenges of Consolidating Democracy in Georgia," *Central Asian Survey* 24, 3 (September 2005): 347.

23. See Richard Giragosian, "Turkmen Human-Rights Commission Convenes Inaugural Meeting," RFE/RL, September 19, 2007, and Liz Fuller, "Turkmen President Outlines Priorities for 2008," RFE/RL, January 2, 2008.

24. Richard Giragosian, "Kazakh President Praises Civil Society," RFE/RL, October 19, 2007; see also Sergei Diachenko, "The Government and NGOs in Kazakhstan: Strategy, Forms, and Mechanisms of Cooperation," *Central Asia and the Caucasus* 43, 1 (2007): 44–56; Richard Weitz, "OSCE Designates Kazakhstan as First Central Asian Presidency," *Central Asia-Caucasus Analyst* (December 12, 2007), http://www.cacianalyst.org.

25. Richard Giragosian, "Kyrgyz Human-Rights Commissioner Apologizes to NGO," RFE/RL, September 6, 2007.

26. Alfred B. Evans Jr., Laura A. Henry, and Lisa McIntosh Sundstrom, eds., *Russian Civil Society: A Critical Assessment* (Armonk, NY: M.E. Sharpe, 2006); Clifford J. Levy, "Russia Denies Visa to Rights Group Leader in Days before Report," *New York Times,* February 21, 2008.

27. Per longtime (and heroic) human rights activist Lev Ponamarev, quoted in Cathy Young, "Freedom and Fear: A Russian Paradox," *Boston Globe,* February 13, 2008.

28. Robert Coalson, "Successor Makes First Campaign Speech," RFE/RL, January 23, 2008.

29. Kelly McMann, *Economic Autonomy and Democracy* (Cambridge: Cambridge University Press, 2006).

II. Politics as Elite Infighting

1. Ralf Dahrendorf pointed this out early on in: "Roads to Freedom: Democratization and Its Problems in East Central Europe," in *Uncertain Futures: Eastern Europe and Democracy,* ed. Peter Vorden (New York: Institute for East-West Security Studies, 1990), 10–13.

2. Again, the Baltic republics were the exception, and Keith Darden and Anna Grzymala-Busse suggest why when they link mass resistance to

and then mobilization against Communism to mass schooling before Communism: "The Great Divide: Literacy, Nationalism, and the Communist Collapse," *World Politics* 59 (October 2006): 83–115.

3. By 2001 only 15 percent of Russia's 1993 business elite was still in place. Olga Kryshtanovskaya and Stephen White, "The Rise of the Russian Business Elite," *Communist and Post-Communist Studies* 38 (2005): 293–307.

4. Robert J. Brym and Vladimir Gimpelson, "The Size, Composition, and Dynamics of the Russian State Bureaucracy in the 1990s," *Slavic Review* 63, 1 (Spring 2004): 109–110. We have the same picture in Kazakhstan; see Jonathan Murphy, "Illusory Transition? Elite Reconstitution in Kazakhstan, 1989–2002," in *Europe-Asia Studies* 58, 4 (June 2006): 523–554.

5. Cited in Walter D. Connor, "Social Change and Stability in Eastern Europe," *Problems of Communism* 26, 6 (November–December 1977): 31.

6. For a summary, see Gail W. Lapidus, "Asymmetrical Federalism and State Breakdown in Russia," *Post-Soviet Affairs* 15, 1 (1999): 74–82.

7. Elise Giuliano, *Why Secession Fails: The Rise and Fall of Ethnic Nationalism in Russia* (Ithaca, NY: Cornell University Press, forthcoming); till then, "The Saliency of Cultural Cleavages: Theorizing Nationalist Separatism in Russia," in *Rebounding Identities: The Politics of Identity in Russia and Ukraine,* ed. Dominique Arel and Blair A. Ruble (Washington, DC: Johns Hopkins University Press, 2006): 33–61; on one aspect, see Dmitry P. Gorenburg, "Tatar Language Policies in Comparative Perspective: Why Some Revivals Fail and Some Succeed," *Ab Imperio* 5, 1: 257–283.

8. As the former Kyrgyzstan foreign minister Roza Otunbayeva put it in 2007, "Russia for us is and remains the outpost of Europe—it provides the link to European values. A dynamic development of a sound democracy in Russia could mean for all CIS countries a real breakthrough to democratic development in the entire region. Russia has been and remains the key country with enormous economic and political influence on our countries. With its economic growth, with the wars of the USA in Iraq and Afghanistan, and tension in US–Iranian relationships, Russia's actual grip on the region gets ever tighter: "We badly need the close attention." Quoted in *IWM Post* (the newsletter of the Institut für die Wissenschaften vom Menschen [Institute for Human Sciences], Vienna) 95 (January–June 2007): 7, http://www.iwm.at. But note the passage from hope to dread in a single paragraph.

9. Some of the flavor of the extensive Western literature of those early years can be gained at two of its high points: Mark R. Beissinger, "The Persisting Ambiguity of Empire," *Post-Soviet Affairs* 11, 2 (April–

June 1995): 149–185, and Ronald Grigor Suny's response, "Ambiguous Categories: States, Empires and Nations," 185–196. Other peaks are to be found in the suggestions for further reading.

10. For a late report, see Richard Giragosian, "Tajikistan to Take Over Leadership of EURASEC," RFE/RL, October 9, 2007.

11. For another late report, see Liz Fuller, "Azerbaijan Hosts GUAM Summit," RFE/RL, June 20, 2007.

12. Richard Giragosian, "Azerbaijani President Characterizes CIS as 'Useless Organization,'" RFE/RL, December 27, 2006; and Igor Torbakov, "The CIS: A Vanishing Reality?" Eurasia Insight, March 7, 2008, http://www.eurasianet.org.

13. Patrick Moore, "Foreign Minister Defends Record in 2007," RFE/RL, January 3, 2008; Moore, "Russia Wants New Security System," RFE/RL, January 24, 2008.

14. See Alexander I. Nikitin, "Post-Soviet Military-Political Integration: The Collective Security Treaty Organization and Its Relations with the EU and NATO," *China and Eurasia Quarterly* 5, 1 (2007): 35–44.

15. Peter D. Wiles, *Communist International Economics* (Oxford: Blackwell, 1968), 311.

16. A warning (retrospective but still early) in Gerald M. Easter, "Preference for Presidentialism: Postcommunist Regime Change in Russia and the NIS," *World Politics* 49 (January 1997): 184–211. On how Moldova has stayed different, see Luke March and Graeme P. Herd, "Moldova between Europe and Russia: Inoculating Against the Colored Contagion?" *Post-Soviet Affairs* 22, 4 (2006): 349–376.

17. Robert Coalson, "Unified Russia Secures Two-Thirds Majority in New Duma," RFE/RL, December 3, 2007; Daniel Kimmage, "Kazakh 'Democratization Task Force' Endorses Presidential System," RFE/RL, February 21, 2007; Kimmage, "Kazakh President Empowered to Remain in Office for Life," RFE/RL, May 22, 2007; Richard Giragosian, "Ruling Kazakh Party Sweeps Parliamentary Election," RFE/RL, August 20, 2007, "Kyrgyz Court Overturns Constitutional Amendments," RFE/RL, September 17, 2007, and "Kyrgyz Officials Announce Four Parties to Enter Parliament," RFE/RL, December 20, 2007; Erica Marat, "Comparing Pro-Presidential Parties in Central Asia," *Central Asia-Caucasus Analyst,* December 12, 2007, http://www.cacianalyst.org.

18. Daniel Kimmage, "Kazakh President Urges Central Asian Union, Gradual Political Change," RFE/RL, April 10, 2007; "Nazarbayev: Reforms in Ukraine Resulted in Instability, the Same Scenario in Kyrgyzstan," *Central Asia-Caucasus Analyst,* April 18, 2007, http://www.cacianalyst.org; Patrick Moore, "Kremlin Aide Compares Putin to F.D.R.," RFE/RL, February 9, 2007; Robert Coalson, "[Putin] Defends Record and Looks to the Future," RFE/RL, October 19, 2007; Coalson,

"Analyst Hopeful about Medvedev's Democratic Leanings," RFE/RL, January 28, 2008, and "Medvedev Emphasizes Need for Strong Presidential Rule," RFE/RL, February 19, 2008.

19. Lucan A. Way, "Rapacious Individualism and Political Competition in Ukraine, 1992–2004," *Communist and Post-Communist Studies* 38 (2005): 191–205; he borrows the term from Martin Shefter writing on premachine New York City politics in the nineteenth century.

20. "The Rise of Competitive Authoritarianism," *Journal of Democracy* 13, 2 (April 2002): 51–65.

21. Anna Zelkina, *In Quest of God and Freedom: The Sufi Response to the Russian Advance in the North Caucasus* (New York: New York University Press, 2000), and now Emil Souleimanov, *An Endless War: The Russian-Chechen Conflict in Perspective* (Frankfurt am Main: Peter Lang, 2007), 127–150.

22. Kathleen Collins, *Clan Politics and Regime Transition in Central Asia* (Cambridge: Cambridge University Press, 2006); Alisher Khamidov, "Kyrgyzstan: Kinship and Patronage Networks Emerge as a Potent Political Force," Commentary, November 21, 2006, http://www.eurasianet .org; and Gulnoza Saidazimova, "New Turkmen President Still Bound to Clan, Nepotism," RFE/RL, October 11, 2007.

23. Jan Maksymiuk, "Ukrainian Ruling Party Proposes Referendum on Russian Language, Neutrality," RFE/RL, September 6, 2007, and "Ukrainian Party Claims to Have Enough Signatures for Referendum," RFE/RL, September 18, 2007; Aleksander Maksymiuk, "Ukraine Accuses Russia of Fueling Language Question," RFE/RL, January 11, 2008.

24. Where the oligarchs came from in Russia is described by my colleague Marshall I. Goldman in *The Piratization of Russia: Russian Reform Goes Awry* (London and New York: Routledge, 2003) and by Stephen Fortescue, *Russia's Oil Barons and Metal Magnates: Oligarchs and the State in Transition* (New York: Palgrave Macmillan, 2006). Anders Åsland now tells us what has happened to them, in *Russia's Capitalist Revolution: Why Market Reform Succeeded and Democracy Failed* (Washington, DC: Peterson Institute for International Economics, 2007).

25. Kirill Nourzhanov, "Saviours of the Nation or Robber Barons? Warlord Politics in Tajikistan," *Central Asian Survey* 24, 2 (June 2005): 109–130; Sabine Freizer, "Neo-liberal and Communal Civil Society in Tajikistan: Merging or Dividing in the Post War Period?" *Central Asian Survey* 24, 3 (September 2005): 225–243; Johan Engval, "Kyrgyzstan: Anatomy of a State," *Problems of Post-Communism* 54, 4 (July–August 2007): 33–45; Alisher Ilkhamov, "Neopatrimonialism, Interest Groups and Patronage Networks," *Central Asian Survey* 26, 1 (March 2007): 65–84; Kimitaka Matsuzato, "A Populist Island in an Ocean of Clan Politics: The Lukashenka Regime as an Exception among CIS Countries," *Europe-*

Asia Studies 56, 2 (March 2004): 235–261; David R. Marples, "Europe's Last Dictatorship: The Roots and Perspectives of Authoritarianism in 'White Russia,'" *Europe-Asia Studies* 57, 6 (September 2005): 895–908; Jan Maksymiuk, "Theories Abound in Ouster of Belarus KGB Chief," RFE/RL, July 24, 2007; Erica Marat, "Nazarbayev Prevails over Political Competitors, Family Members," *Central-Asia Caucasus Analyst,* May 5, 2007, http://www.cacianalyst.org; Joanna Lillis, "Kazakhstan: President's Daughter to Sit Out the Upcoming Election," Eurasia Insight, July 17, 2007, http://www.eurasianet.org; Robert Coalson, "Speculation on War among Siloviki Intensifies," RFE/RL, October 10, 2007; Jonas Bernstein, "Russian President Tells Security Services to Behave," RFE/RL, December 21, 2007; but see Coalson, "Siloviki Form Strong Bloc in New Duma," RFE/RL, December 28, 2007.

26. Henry E. Hale, "Regime Cycles: Democracy, Autocracy, and Revolution in Post-Soviet Eurasia," *World Politics* 58 (October 2005): 133–165. See also C. J. Chivers, "How Top Spies in Ukraine Changed the Nation's Path," *New York Times,* January 17, 2005. In fact, one reason the color revolutions have not turned out so wonderfully is that they were "initiated, led, controlled, and finally subordinated by former members of the authoritarian regimes' political elite": Theodor Tudoroiu, "Rose, Orange, and Tulip: The Failed Post-Soviet Revolutions," *Communist and Post-Communist Studies* 40 (2007): 315–342. Tudoroiu's analysis uncannily reflects Romania's experience in and after 1989, in which many saw a "revolution" hijacked by its post-Communist perpetrators. For a (characteristically) more fine-grained analysis of Ukraine's Orange Revolution, which shows elite splits to be just one of the factors but (characteristically) overstates the external role, see Michael McFaul, "Ukraine Imports Democracy: External Influences on the Orange Revolution," *International Security* 32, 2 (Fall 2007): 45–83.

27. Liz Fuller, "Senior Officials, Parliamentarians Defect to Former Armenian President's Camp," RFE/RL, February 25, 2008; "Armenia: Uneasy Quiet Settles over Yerevan: Residents in Shock over Use of Force by Kocharian Administration," Armenia: Vote 2008, March 2, 2008, http://www.eurasianet.org.

28. Compared with Georgia and Ukraine, Kyrgyzstan's Tulip Revolution featured more poor people and fewer NGOs, but these poor were still organized by elite networks, especially in the south. See Matthew Fuhrmann, "A Tale of Two Social Capitals: Revolutionary Collective Action in Kyrgyzstan," *Problems of Post-Communism* 53, 6 (November–December 2006): 16–29.

III. The Politics of Economics and Sovereignty

1. Daniel Kimmage, "Turkmen Leader Readies Mercedes, Jeeps for Officials," RFE/RL, August 8, 2006; and Kimmage, "and Sacks Two Governors for Cotton-Harvest Lapses," RFE/RL, October 27, 2006.

2. LB, "Oligarch to Build World's Biggest Yacht," RFE/RL, August 30, 2005; Robert Coalson, "Abramovich Buys Airbus A380," RFE/RL, September 6, 2007; Coalson, "Deripaska Heads List of Russian Billionaires," RFE/RL, February 19, 2008; and Coalson, "Russians Make Leap Forward on Global Billionaires' List," March 7, 2008: as of that writing there were 87 Russian billionaires (with an average age 46) including 19 of the top 100 richest people in the world, second only to the U.S. (whose billionaires' average age was 61).

3. Patrick Moore, "Former Yukos Director Tells of Bizarre Life on the Inside," RFE/RL, August 7, 2006.

4. Rawi Abdelal, *National Purpose in the World Economy: Post-Soviet States in Comparative Perspective* (Ithaca, NY: Cornell University Press, 2001).

5. Yoshiko Herrera, *Imagined Economies: The Sources of Russian Regionalism* (Cambridge: Cambridge University Press, 2005).

6. See Gail W. Lapidus, "Asymmetrical Federalism and State Breakdown in Russia," *Post-Soviet Affairs* 15, 1 (1999): 74–82.

7. Marshall I. Goldman, *Petrostate: Putin, Power, and the New Russia* (Oxford: Oxford University Press, 2008), 145–149; Margarita M. Balmaceda, *Energy Dependency, Politics and Corruption in the Former Soviet Union: Russia's Power, Oligarchs' Profits and Ukraine's Missing Energy Policy, 1995–2006* (New York: Routledge, 2008); and now her "Understanding the Comparative Management of Energy Dependency in the Former Soviet World" (discussion paper for a workshop on post-Communist politics and economics, Harvard University, February 25, 2008). Cited by permission of the author. The shady intermediaries may disappear at some point—see Aleksander Maksymiuk, "Ukraine, Russia Sign Agreement on Direct Gas Supplies," RFE/RL, March 14, 2008—but they may not.

8. Gerald M. Easter, "Politics of Revenue Extraction in Post-Communist States: Poland and Russia Compared," *Politics and Society* 30, 4 (December 2002): 599–627; Pauline Jones Luong and Erika Weinthal, "Contra Coercion: Russian Tax Reform, Exogenous Shocks, and Negotiated Institutional Change," *American Political Science Review* 98, 1 (February 2004): 139–152; Easter, "Building Fiscal Capacity," in *The State after Communism: Governance in the New Russia,* ed. Timothy J. Colton and Stephen Holmes (Lanham, MD: Rowman & Littlefield, 2006), 21–52; Anders Åslund, "Postrevolutionary Stabilization: 1999–2003," *Russia's Capi-*

talist Revolution (Washington, DC: Peterson Institute for International Economics, 2007), 189–199.

9. Goldman tells the whole story with his usual clarity in *Petrostate;* see also Åslund, *Russia's Capitalist Revolution,* 210, and his fine summing up on this doomed period, "The Oligarchy: 1996–1998," 157–187.

10. "Anatoly Chubais: Russia Should Aim to Create Liberal Empire in CIS," *Pravda,* September 25, 2003, http://www.newsfromrussia.com/2003/09/35/50165.html; and Igor Torbakov, "Russian Policymakers Air Notion of 'Liberal Empire' in Caucasus, Central Asia," Eurasia Insight, October 27, 2003, http://www.eurasianet.org.

11. Gregory Gleason, "Russia and the Politics of the Central Asian Electricity Grid," *Problems of Post-Communism* 50, 3 (May/June 2003): 42–52.

12. Robert Coalson, "Putin Elite Consolidates Its Position in Business Circles," RFE/RL, February 6, 2008.

13. Åslund, "Renationalization: The Creation of Kremlin, Inc." in *Capitalist Revolution,* 250–259.

14. Robert Coalson, "Kremlin Official Says Yukos Case Is Lesson to Other Businesses," RFE/RL, March 29, 2005. Or as Voltaire famously remarked when the British shot Admiral John Byng for failing to relieve Minorca in 1757, it was "to encourage the others."

15. Patrick Moore, "Over Half of State Budget from Hydrocarbon Revenues," RFE/RL, August 18, 2006; Christopher Walker, "The Emerging Post-Soviet Petrostates," RFE/RL, February 2, 2007; Åslund, *Capitalist Revolution,* 270–271.

16. VY, "Putin Expresses Chagrin over Economic Figures," RFE/RL, June 15, 2005; Brian Whitmore, "[Putin] Reiterates Goal of Doubling GDP by 2010," RFE/RL, May 20, 2006; Jonas Bernstein, "[Putin] Reiterates Russia's development goals," RFE/RL, February 14, 2008: Those goals now include building up Russia's middle class from 20 to 55 percent of the population by 2020.

17. All from RFE/RL *Newsline:* Robert Coalson, "Putin Creates New State Megacorporation" (for machine-building), November 27, 2007; Patrick Moore, "Putin Signs Law on Rosatom" (for nuclear energy), December 3, 2007; Coalson, "Putin Pledges to Reform State Corporations," December 12, 2007; Jonas Bernstein, "[Putin] . . . Removing Administrative Barriers," February 15, 2008.

18. Harley Balzer, "Vladimir Putin's Academic Writings and Russian National Resource Policy," in *Problems of Post-Communism* 53, 1 (January/February 2006): 48–54.

19. Brian Whitmore, "President Praises State's 'Purposefui Work' with Gazprom," RFE/RL, May 10, 2006. Also: Patrick Moore, "No Privatization for Russian Railways," RFE/RL, August 1, 2007.

20. Moldovans tended to see the bans as punishment for tighter border controls on breakaway Trans-Dniestria, which hosts Russian troops. Even after the bans were lifted in 2006 and 2007 following Moldovan support for Russia's accession to the World Trade Organization (WTO), there was obscure foot-dragging: see Andrew Gardner, "Russia Orders Lifting of Wine Ban on Moldova," RFE/RL, June 25, 2007, which includes citations on the other bans; and Gardner, "Moldova Says Russia Should Open Door to All Wine or None," RFE/RL, July 27, 2007.

21. VY, "Duma Deputy Calls for Raising Price of Gas for Georgia and Calls on Government to Do Same for other 'Disloyal' States"; and "[Putin] Promises to Expand Gas Exports," RFE/RL, July 11, 2005.

22. Balmaceda, *Energy Dependency,* gives a convenient account of the crisis.

23. The following articles are all by Patrick Moore in RFE/RL *Newsline* on the date given: "Russia Takes Stock of G8," July 18, 2006; "Putin Aide Says Munich Speech Was Aimed at Sympathetic Europeans," February 23, 2007; "Minister Rejects Criticism of Russian Foreign Policy," April 7, 2006; "Foreign Ministry Says Russia Is Force for Good in World," March 28, 2007.

24. Again by Patrick Moore in RFE/RL *Newsline:* "Russia Tests New ICBM that Can Beat 'Any System,'" May 30, 2007; "Russian Explorers Plant Titanium Flag at North Pole," August 3, 2007; "Putin Announces Resumption of Strategic Bomber Flights," August 20, 2007; "Russian Navy Will Return to Atlantic, Mediterranean," December 6, 2007; "Russia Test-Fires, Deploys ICBMs," December 17, 2007; "Russia Again Threatens to Target Poland, Czech Republic with Missiles," December 18, 2007; "Russian Media Hail Muscle-Flexing," August 21, 2007; "Putin Says Russia Is Becoming Stronger," January 2, 2008.

25. Patrick Moore, "[Putin] Denies Russia Uses Energy for Political Leverage," RFE/RL, January 30, 2008.

26. To take just the Estonian example, already after Putin's Munich speech President Toomas Hendrik Ilves had declared Russia "a country that considers democracy on its borders as a threat, (and) despotism inside its borders as a source of stability," and when Estonia then outraged Russia by moving the monument to the Soviet soldiers out of central Tallinn, there followed (in addition to the siege of its Moscow Embassy) cuts in Russian energy supplies, massive cyber attacks on Estonian government computers, canceled rail service, strangled truck traffic, cuts in energy transiting Estonia from Russia, and finally a ban on Estonian poultry. All from RFE/RL *Newsline:* Patrick Moore, "Estonian President Feels Vindicated by Putin's Speech," February 13, 2007; Jonas Bernstein, "Russia Cuts Energy Supplies to Estonia," May 3, 2007; Floriana Fossato, "Russian Railways Cancel Services between St. Petersburg and Tallinn," May 9,

156   *Notes to Pages 84–87*

2007; Fossato, "Russia Restricts Traffic over Bridge to Estonia," May 10, 2007; Bernstein, "Estonia Reportedly Target of 'Massive Cyber-Attacks,'" May 21, 2007; Moore, "Russia Reportedly Moves to Cut Shipments to Estonia," July 17, 2007; Moore, "Russia Restricts Poultry Imports from Estonia," May 21, 2007. Estonia did not yield; as Churchill said of the French prediction that Britain would have its neck wrung like a chicken in 1940, "Some chicken. Some neck." Yet it could be forgiven for seeing the point as political.

27. Patrick Moore, "Russia Calls Lithuanian Railway Shutdown 'Provocative,'" RFE/RL, August 29, 2006.

28. Patrick Moore, "Lithuania Says Russia Is Delaying Pipeline Repairs," RFE/RL, August 8, 2006.

29. Marshall I. Goldman sorts all these gas pipelines out masterfully in *Petrostate,* 152–162.

30. The great stories of 2006 and 2007 were renegotiation of Russia's $20 billion Sakhalin-2 gas project to give Gazprom 50 percent plus one share, and Kazakhstan's renegotiation of the contract to exploit the Kashagan oil field, with its estimated 13 billion barrels, to boost the state oil company's share. Kyrgyzstan also upped its take (and social spending from) the massive Kumtor gold mine. See Patrick Moore, "Gazprom Takes Control of Sakhalin-2 from Shell," RFE/RL, December 22, 2006; Joanna Lillis, "Oil Companies on the Defensive in Kazakhstan," Business and Economics, October 10, 2007, http://www.eurasianet.org; Lillis, "Kazakhstan: Officials Jubilant over Oil-Field Renegotiation Deal," ibid., January 23, 2008; and then: Richard Giragosian, "Kazakh Premier Announces End to Production-Sharing Contracts in Mining Sector," RFE/RL, February 22, 2008. For the Kyrgyz version of forced contract adjustment: Daniel Sershen, "Rethinking Kyrgyzstan's Gold Profits," Business and Economics, March 8, 2007, http://www.eurasianet.org, and Nurshat Ababakirov, "Kyrgyz Kumtor Mine Controversy Heats Up," *Central Asia-Caucasus Analyst,* March 5, 2008, http://www.cacianalyst.org.

31. Robert Coalson, "Another Billionaire Ready to Give Everything to the State," RFE/RL, October 2, 2007; the $40 billion figure comes from Coalson, "Deripaska Heads List," RFE/RL, February 19, 2008.

32. Coalson, "Tax Service to Turn Its Attention to the Oligarchs," RFE/RL, September 26, 2007.

33. This Stabilization Fund has a story of its own. On closing it was split into a $125 billion Reserve Fund and a second $32 billion entity to function as a sovereign wealth fund investing in corporate bonds and shares. Putin had after all declared to President Nicholas Sarkozy of France the previous fall that "it is [an] absolutely honest, transparent and mutually acceptable approach for our companies to buy into their European partners and for European partners to acquire stakes in Russian com-

panies, which creates a situation of interdependence and mutual control."
While "campaigning" to replace Putin, Medvedev chimed in that of course
Russian business needs a strong state. Sure enough, businessmen across
the country joined officials in lobbying for bits from the new pot. Russia
exempts Gazprom from foreign investment as a strategic monopoly, however, and Europeans bridled at being bought when they cannot buy: as
the chairman of the Eurogroup of finance ministers put it, "It is unacceptable that while Russia's government-affiliated fund is sweeping into
Europe, European companies are in a situation where they are unable to
conduct similar activities in Russia." He may not have found "mutual control" with Putin very appealing either. Russia's first deputy prime minister Sergei Ivanov had already answered a similar American charge ten
months before: "You taught us how to be a . . . market economy. We
learned our lesson." Others were not so sure a market economy was what
they were looking at. See Robert Coalson, "Stabilization Fund Closed,
Two New Funds Created," RFE/RL, February 1, 2008; Patrick Moore,
"France Wants Stake in Gazprom, Putin Likes 'Mutual Control,'" RFE/
RL, October 11, 2007; Moore, "Medvedev Calls on Russians to Invest
Abroad," and Coalson, "The Pot of Gold at the End of Russia's Stabiliza-
tion Fund," both RFE/RL, February 1, 2008; Moore, "EU Raps Russia
Over Sovereign Wealth Fund," RFE/RL, February 7, 2008; Moore, "Is
Gazprom Playing 'Monopoly?'" RFE/RL, April 19, 2007.

    34. All from RFE/RL *Newsline:* Patrick Moore, "Russian Purchase of
U.S. Steel Firm Reportedly Set to Go Ahead," January 10, 2007; Moore,
"Russian Tycoon Buys Hungary's Airline," February 26, 2007; Andrew
Gardner, "Montenegro's Former President Unconcerned by Russian Eco-
nomic Influence," May 2, 2007; on Luxembourg, Moore, "Putin Seeks to
Split Europe," May 25, 2007. All the following by Patrick Moore in RFE/
RL *Newsline:* "Russian Airline Drops Out of Race to Take over Italian
Competitor," June 28, 2007; "Is Russia Preparing to Sell Its Stake in [Air-
bus parent] EADS?" July 12, 2007; "Russia Reduces Oil Exports to Ger-
many," August 27, 2007; "Russian Oil Firm Reaches Deal with Germany,"
August 29, 2007; "EU Draws the Line for Gazprom . . . and Russia Is Not
Amused," September 20, 2007; "Gazprom Buys Storage Site near Berlin,"
November 28, 2007; "Renault to Buy Quarter of Russia's Biggest Car
Maker," December 10, 2007; "Russia Cashes in on Its Political Support for
Serbia," January 28, 2008. Richard Giragosian, "Uzbek President Ap-
proves General Motors Investment," RFE/RL, March 10, 2008.

    35. On the 2007–8 round, all from RFE/RL *Newsline:* Richard Gi-
ragosian, "Russian Gazprom Head Agrees to Price Hike for Turkmen
Gas Supplies," November 28, 2007; Aleksander Maksymiuk, "Gazprom,
Ukraine Set Gas Price for 2008," December 5, 2007; Patrick Moore,
"Three Presidents [of Russia, Kazakhstan, and Turkmenistan] Sign Gas

Pipeline Agreement [to skirt the Caspian to Russia]," December 21, 2007; Giragosian, "Tajikistan Reaches Price Agreement for Imports of Uzbek Natural Gas," December 28, 2007; Giragosian, "Kyrgyz Official Announces . . . New Agreement on Gas Imports from Uzbekistan," January 11, 2008; Giragosian, "Uzbekistan Cuts Gas Supplies to Tajikistan," January 25, 2008"; Giragosian, "Kazakhstan Raises Tariffs for Russian Gas Shipments," February 5, 2008; Liz Fuller, "Azerbaijan to Raise Price for Natural Gas" (for the Russians are not the only tough kids on the block); Aleksander Maksymiuk, "Ukrainian, Russian Premiers Back Presidents' Gas Agreements," February 21, 2008.

36. All from RFE/RL *Newsline:* Patrick Moore, "[Putin] Aide . . . Defends Current Policies," June 29, 2006; Moore, "Russia Sets Foreign-Policy Priorities for 'Self-Confident' State," March 29, 2007; Patrick Moore and Liz Fuller, "Putin Calls for Russian 'Moratorium' on Implementing Arms Treaty," April 26, 2007; Moore, "Key Legislator Says Nobody Will 'Twist Russia's Arm' on World Markets," October 2, 2007; Moore, "Putin Says 'Russia Is Not Iraq,' Can Defend Itself," October 19, 2007; Moore, "Putin Slams Those Who Want 'to Split Russia,'" November 5, 2007; the same, "Putin Accepts U.S. Distinction by Blasting U.S.," December 20, 2007; Jonas Bernstein, "Putin Trashes 1990s, Praises Last Eight Years," February 11, 2008; Moore, "[Putin] Says He Fears Encirclement," February 13, 2008.

IV. States, Nations, and Nationalisms in Eurasia

1. Mark Mazower, *Dark Continent: Europe's Twentieth Century* (New York: Knopf, 1998).

2. Dmitry P. Gorenburg, "Soviet Nationalities Policy and Assimilation" in *Rebounding Identities: The Politics of Identity in Russia and Ukraine,* ed. Dominique Arel and Blair A. Ruble (Baltimore: Johns Hopkins University Press, 2006), 273–303.

3. Geoffrey A. Hosking, *Russia: People and Empire, 1552–1917* (Cambridge, MA: Harvard University Press, 1997).

4. Ronald Grigor Suny, "Ambiguous Categories: States, Empires, and Nations," *Post-Soviet Affairs* 11, 2 (April–June 1995): 191.

5. Again, Mark R. Beissinger, "The Persisting Ambiguity of Empire," *Post-Soviet Affairs* 11, 2 (April–June 1995): 150, 163.

6. Andrei V. Korobkov and Zhanna A. Zaionchkovskaia, "The Changes in the Migration Patterns in the Post-Soviet States: The First Decade," *Communist and Post-Communist Studies* 37 (2004): 481–508, and Anne White, "Internal Migration Trends in Soviet and Post-Soviet European Russia," *Europe-Asia Studies* 59, 6 (September 2007): 887–911. Mi-

grants' remittances can be hugely important to the smaller economies: see Daniel Kimmage, "Uzbek Migrant Workers Add $1 Billion to Economy," RFE/RL, June 21, 2007; or 8 percent of Uzbekistan's GDP.

7. Looking back from 2007, Uzbekistan's President Karimov remembered how in the beginning he had to "re-create" almost every ministry and department: see Aftab Kazi, "Dealing with Uzbekistan after Karimov's Likely Re-Election," *Central Asia-Caucasus Analyst,* December 12, 2007, http://www.cacianalyst.org.

8. On Central Asia, see Adeeb Khalid, *Islam after Communism: Religion and Politics in Central Asia* (Berkeley: University of California Press, 2007). I teach a course in Harvard's government department on post-Communist Islam that covers all the post-Soviet areas plus the Balkans.

9. All from RFE/RL *Newsline:* Brian Whitmore, "Russian President Calls for Revival of Traditional Culture," December 29, 2006; Patrick Moore, "Putin Hails 'Moral Values' to Mark Russian Orthodox Christmas," January 8, 2007; Floriana Fossato, "Russian Orthodox Churches Reunite," May 17, 2007; Robert Coalson, "Putin Urges Orthodox to Vote," November 20, 2007.

10. Patrick Moore, "Putin Says Russia Has No Territorial Ambitions," RFE/RL, June 5, 2006.

11. Sébastien Peyrouse, "Christianity and Nationality in Soviet and Post-Soviet Central Asia: Mutual Intrusions and Instrumentalizations," *Nationalities Papers* 32, 3 (September 2004): 651–674.

12. See Zvi Gitelman, ed., *Jewish Life after the USSR* (Bloomington: Indiana University Press, 2003).

13. Kate Graney, "Making Russia Multicultural: Kazan at Its Millennium and Beyond," *Problems of Post-Communism* 54, 6 (November/December 2007): 17–27; Olessia Vovina, "Islam and the Creation of Sacred Space: The Mishar Tatars of Chuvashia," *Religion, State & Society* 34, 3 (September 2006): 255–269; Marlène Laruelle, "Tengrism: In Search of Central Asia's Spiritual Roots," *Central Asia-Caucasus Analyst,* March 22, 2006, http://www.cacianalyst.org; Gitelman, *Jewish Life,* 50.

14. For that story through 2004, see Joan F. Chevalier, "Language Policy in the Russian Federation: Russian as the 'State Language,'" *Ab Imperio* (2005/1): 285–303.

15. Joldosh Osmonov, "Uzbek Community in Kyrgyzstan Want Uzbek as Official Language," *Central Asia-Caucasus Analyst,* June 14, 2006, http://www.cacianalyst.org; Daniel Kimmage, "Kyrgyz Legislators Reject Official Status for Uzbek Language," RFE/RL, March 27, 2007.

16. Victoria Clement, "Alphabet Changes in Turkmenistan, 1904–2004," in *Everyday Life in Central Asia: Past and Present,* ed. Jeff Sahadeo and Russell Zanca (Bloomington: Indiana University Press, 2007), 266–

280; Paul Bartlett, "Kazakhstan: Moving Forward with Plan to Replace Cyrillic with Latin Alphabet," Civil Society, September 4, 2007, http://www.eurasianet.org.

17. Steven D. Roper, "The Politicization of Education: Identity Formation in Moldova and Transnistria," *Communist and Post-Communist Studies* 38 (2005): 501–514.

18. Jan Maksymiuk, "Belarusian President's Website Launches Belarusian-Language Version," RFE/RL, June 28, 2007; Richard Giragosian, "Kyrgyz President Reviews Economic Situation on Regional Tour," RFE/RL, October 18, 2007; William Fierman, "Kazakh Language and Prospects for Its Role in Kazakh 'Groupness,'" *Ab Imperio* (2005/2): 393–421; Daniel Kimmage, "Report Says Education Reform Under Way in Turkmenistan [i.e., to boost the teaching of Russian]," RFE/RL, February 27, 2007; Kimmage, "Kazakh Constitutional Court Decrees Equality of Kazakh, Russian Languages," RFE/RL, February 27, 2007; Richard Weitz, "Central Asia: Looking at Language Politics" (report on a Fierman talk), Civil Society, January 28, 2008, http://www.eurasianet.org.

19. That is only one option; David Laitin reviews a number of others, including formation of a "Russian-speaking nationality" outside Russia: *Identity in Formation: The Russian-Speaking Populations in the Near Abroad* (Ithaca, NY: Cornell University Press, 1998). But that does not seem to be the direction Russians outside Russia are heading.

20. Oxana Shevel, "Nationality in Ukraine: Some Rules of Engagement," *East European Politics and Societies* 16, 2 (2002): 386–413; Dominique Arel, "Interpreting 'Nationality' and 'Language' in the 2001 Ukrainian Census," *Post-Soviet Affairs* 18, 3 (2002): 213–249; Stephen Shulman, "The Contours of Civic and Ethnic National Identification in Ukraine," *Europe-Asia Studies* 56, 1 (January 2004): 35–56.

21. Patrick Moore, "Ministry Plans to Repatriate 300,000 Russians," RFE/RL, July 24, 2006; Moore, "Putin Vows to Implement Repatriation Project," RFE/RL, October 25, 2006; Dmitry Shlapentokh, "Kondopoga, 'Russian March' and After: The Russian Authorities' Response to the Rise of Russian Nationalism," *Central Asia-Caucasus Analyst,* February 7, 2007, http://www.cacianalyst.org; Patrick Moore, "New Law Banning Foreign Salespeople Takes Effect," RFE/RL, April 2, 2007; Jonas Bernstein, "Racist Attacks on the Rise," RFE/RL, May 3, 2007; Richard Giragosian, "Kyrgyz Officials Express Concern over Hate Crimes Targeting Kyrgyz Nationals in Russia," RFE/RL, February 19, 2008.

22. Both from RFE/RL *Newsline:* Robert Coalson, "Repatriation Plan Yields Meager Results," December 13, 2007; Patrick Moore, "Russia Wants Its Germans Back," September 12, 2007.

23. The prickly Uzbekistan state under Karimov has been remarkably careful not to use or sponsor Uzbeks in neighboring countries; it just

wants to control its own: Matteo Fumagalli, "Ethnicity, State Formation and Foreign Policy: Uzbekistan and 'Uzbeks Abroad,'" *Central Asian Survey* 26, 1 (March 2007): 105–122.

24. Patrick Moore, "Kremlin Theoretician Wants 'National Ideology,'" RFE/RL, August 31, 2006.

25. It can also underpin muscular Russian policies in the near abroad. Dmitry Trenin was probably a little premature in 2002 when he argued, albeit brilliantly, that such policies are a thing of the past: *The End of Eurasia: Russia on the Border between Geopolitics and Globalization* (Washington, DC: Carnegie Endowment for International Peace, 2002). On the ideology, see VY, "Putin, Shaimiev Hail Eurasianism," RFE/RL, August 29, 2005, Matthew Schmidt, "Is Putin Pursuing a Policy of Eurasianism?" *Demokratizatsya* 13, 1 (Winter 2005): 87–99, and now Dmitry Shlapentokh, "Dugin, Eurasianism, and Central Asia," *Communist and Post-Communist Studies* 40 (2007): 143–156.

26. All from RFE/RL *Newsline:* Patrick Moore, "Senior Leader Rejects 'Sovereign Democracy,'" July 24, 2006; Robert Coalson, "More Details Emerge from Putin's Discussion with Valdai Club," September 21, 2007; Coalson, "Scholars to Study 'Sovereign Democracy,'" December 10, 2007.

27. Victor Yasmann, "Russian Nationalist Writer [Aleksandr Prokhanov] Calls for New 'Eurasian Empire,'" RFE/RL, November 6, 2006; Paradorn Rangsimaporn, "Interpretations of Eurasianism: Justifying Russia's Role in East Asia," *Europe-Asia Studies* 58, 3 (May 2006): 371–389. By far the best and most stimulating study is Marlène Laruelle, *La quête d'une identité impériale: Le néo-eurasisme dans la Russie contemporaine* (Paris: Petra, 2007).

28. Patrick Moore, "Kremlin Theoretician . . . " (see note 24).

29. Two by Patrick Moore from RFE/RL *Newsline:* "Putin Says Russia Wants Good Relations with EU on Its Own Terms," March 26, 2007, and "Russian Daily Notes Minister's 'Pragmatic' Approach," January 24, 2008; Lincoln Mitchell, "What Was the Rose Revolution For? *Harvard International Review* (February 2008), www.harvardir.org/articles/print .php?article=1684; Robert Coalson, "Khakamada Describes Russia's 'Instrumental Democracy,'" RFE/RL, September 19, 2007.

30. Antoine Buisson, "State-Building, Power-Building and Political Legitimacy: The Case of Post-Conflict Tajikistan," *China and Eurasia Forum Quarterly* 5, 4 (November 2007): 115–145.

31. It is possible to theorize "the state" (like "the nation," "the empire" and every other institution) almost to death, till it almost disappears into thin air. My friend David Ludden of NYU appears to be trying to do this, or so I deduce from his working paper on "Topographies of Globalization" presented to Harvard's Workshop on the Political Economy of Modern

Capitalism on March 10, 2008, available at http://www.fas.harvard.edu/
~polecon/Ludden.pdf (cited by permission of the author). Such theorizing may be an American thing, but Frenchmen and Germans do it too, so
I do not think so. Having spent 35 years working for "the (American)
state" I may exaggerate its capacity for good, and I certainly know how little esteem it enjoys in our political culture, compared with Europe's. But
most Americans still grant the state a "thingness" that is missing in much
recent scholarship. I was once trying to cadge a government rate in a Du-
rango, Colorado, motel, and when the clerk asked what part of the government I worked for and I answered the State Department, the reply was
"state department of what?" She knew the state was there—rather than
at some intersection of verticality and horizontality—even if she did not
recognize my bit of it. That is the way I treat it in this book.

32. All from RFE/RL *Newsline* and by Richard Giragosian unless
otherwise stated, "U.S. to Provide Counterterrorism Training to Tajik
Border Troops," January 26, 2007; Patrick Moore, "EU, NATO Hail Signing of Russian-Latvian [Border] Treaty," March 28, 2007; Giragosian,
"Kyrgyzstan Upgrades Checkpoint on Uzbek Border," April 4, 2007; "Kazakh Defense Minister Reports on Naval Buildup," October 31, 2007;
"Kazakhstan Reinforces Security along Uzbek Border," November 1,
2007; "NATO Envoy Pledges to Assist Creation of Kazakh Navy," November 2, 2007; "French Official Visits Kazakhstan, Pledges Aid to
Kazakh Navy," November 6, 2007; "Kyrgyz President Discusses Border
Demarcation with Kazakh Minister," November 14, 2007. For Kazakh-
stan, thickening military cooperation with the West also has a counterbal-
ancing function: Marat Murgaliev, "Kazakh-U.S. Military-Political
Cooperation in the Context of U.S. Geopolitical Interests in Central Asia,"
Central Asia and the Caucasus 44, 2 (2007): 52–61.

33. Edward Schatz, "Transnational Image Making and Soft Author-
itarian Kazakhstan," *Slavic Review* 67, 1 (Spring 2008): 50–62; Robert A.
Saunders, "Buying into Brand Borat: Kazakhstan's Cautious Embrace of
Its Unwanted 'Son,'" ibid., 63–80; David L. Stern, "A Wandering
Kazakh, Before Borat," *New York Times,* February 24, 2008; Laura L.
Adams, *The Spectacular State: Culture and National Identity in Uzbekistan*
(Durham, NC: Duke University Press, forthcoming); Erica Marat,
"Branding the New Nations of Central Asia and South Caucasus," *Cen-
tral Asia-Caucasus Analyst,* November 14, 2007, http://www.cacianalyst
.org.

34. Alexander Cooley, "Imperial Wreckage: Property Rights, Sovereignty, and Security in the Post-Soviet Space," *International Security* 25, 2
(Winter 2000–1): 100–127. In the middle range come issues of dual citizenship. These can be sensitive and vexing, but they still fall in the category of post-Soviet dilemmas to be worked on with practical goodwill: see

Igor Torbakov, "Turkmenistan's Move to Eliminate Dual Citizenship Creates Political Problems for Russian President," Eurasia Insight, June 4, 2003, http://www.eurasianet.org; and Emil Danielyan, "Armenia Allows Dual Citizenship amid Controversy," Civil Society, February 26, 2007, http://www.eurasianet.org.

35. All from RFE/RL *Newsline:* Richard Giragosian, "Official Says More Kyrgyz Acquiring Russian Citizenship," July 12, 2007; Andrew Gardner, "Moldova Protests Russian Polling Stations in Transdniester," November 30, 2007; Liz Fuller, "Abkhazia, South Ossetia Vote in Duma Elections," December 3, 2007. On the Russian voters in Abkhazia and South Ossetia, Foreign Minister Lavrov had earlier explained mildly that they had Russian passports only to give them legal status somewhere, since they are outside the Georgian legal system: see Fuller, "Russian Foreign Minister Discusses Relations with Georgia," February 28, 2007.

36. All from RFE/RL *Newsline:* Andrew Gardner, "Moldova Criticizes Romanian Citizenship Policy," March 8, 2007; Gardner, "Moldovans Overwhelmingly Support EU Membership," May 30, 2007; Aleksander Maksymiuk, "Belarus Worried about 'Polish Charter,'" February 11, 2008.

37. Mark Beissinger has pointed out how strong ethnonationalism was on the Soviet periphery in the run-up to the collapse, and how weak it was among Russians: Mark R. Beissinger, *Nationalist Mobilization and the Collapse of the Soviet State* (Cambridge: Cambridge University Press, 2002). That distinction appears to have held since.

38. Even so, the annual squabble over gas prices since 2006 has probably stiffened Belarusian resistance: see Aleksander Maksymiuk, "Belarusian Lawmaker Says Belarus, Russia See Integration in Different Ways," RFE/RL, February 15, 2008. Balmaceda finds that when it comes to gas negotiations with Russia, Belarus has in fact been more pugnacious than Ukraine: Margarita M. Balmaceda, "Understanding the Comparative Management of Energy Dependency in the Former Soviet World" (discussion paper for a workshop on post-Communist politics and economics, Harvard University, February 25, 2008); cited by permission of the author.

39. Even the weak can push back: see Richard Giragosian, "Kyrgyzstan Temporarily Cuts Electricity for Russian Base," RFE/RL, August 29, 2007.

40. Walter D. Connor, "A Russia That Can Say 'No'?" *Communist and Post-Communist Studies* 40 (2007): 383–391.

V. Today's Eurasia and the United States

1. Edmund Burke, *Reflections on the Revolution in France,* cited in Ross J. S. Hoffman and Paul Levack, eds., *Burke's Politics* (New York: Knopf, 1959), 302.

2, For instance, see Celeste A. Wallander, "U.S.–Russian Relations: Between Realism and Reality," *Current History* 102, 666 (October 2003): 307–312; or Sarah E. Mendelson, "Wanted: A New U.S. Policy on Russia," PONARS Policy Memo no. 324, January 2004, http://www.csis.org/media/csis/pubs/pm_0324.pdf.

3. *Russia's Wrong Direction: What the United States Can and Should Do,* ed. Stephen Sestanovich, Independent Task Force Report sponsored by the Council on Foreign Relations, March 2006, http://www.cfr.org/content/publications/attachments/Russia_TaskForce.pdf.

4. Steven Lee Myers, "Cheney Rebukes Russia on Rights at Europe Forum," *New York Times,* May 5, 2006; Thom Shanker and Mark Landler, "Putin Says U.S. Is Undermining Global Stability," *New York Times,* February 11, 2007; Patrick Moore, "Putin Slams U.S. in Major Speech, Says Russia Will Determine Its Own Future," RFE/RL, February 12, 2007.

5. C. J. Chivers, "The Cure for Chilling Words Could Be a Cooler Temper," *New York Times,* May 13, 2007; Thom Shanker, "Administration Rebukes Putin on His Policies," *New York Times,* June 1, 2007; Sheryl Gay Stolberg, "Chastising Putin, Bush Says Russia Derails Reform," *New York Times,* June 6, 2007.

6. Jonas Bernstein, "Putin Says 'Interference' in Domestic Affairs Is 'Unacceptable,'" RFE/RL, July 3, 2007; Patrick Moore, "U.S. Says Talk of New Cold War with Russia Is 'Nonsense,'" RFE/RL, January 24, 2008.

7. Dmitry Trenin, "Why Russia and America Need Each Other" (lecture, the Kennan Institute, Washington, DC, February 2, 2007), www.wilsoncenter.org/index.cfm?fuseaction=topics.event_summary&event_id=215228; and Rose Gottemoeller, "Reading Russia Right," *New York Times,* May 4, 2007 (just before Putin linked U.S. policy with Hitler's).

8. Patrick Moore, "U.S. Ambassador Calls for 'Strategic Dialogue' with Russia," RFE/RL, March 2, 2007, and "Key U.S. Senator [Richard Lugar] Calls for Steps to Improve 'Complicated' Relationship," RFE/RL, October 9, 2007.

9. Thom Shanker and Helene Cooper, "U.S. Moves to Soothe Growing Russian Resentment," *New York Times,* March 5, 2007; Floriana Fossato, "Russia, U.S. Agree Only to Tone Down Rhetoric," RFE/RL, May 16, 2007; Jonas Bernstein, "Ivanov Speaks Softly at Munich Security Conference," RFE/RL, February 11, 2008; Patrick Moore, "Russia Slams U.S. over Sanctions [on arms exporters]," RFE/RL, January 8, 2007; Moore, "U.S. Says Russia Is Planning a Ban on U.S. Pork, Chicken Exports," RFE/RL, October 22, 2007 ("Russia is reportedly the largest overseas buyer of U.S. chicken"); Bernstein, "U.S. and Russia Reach Agreement on Plutonium Disposal Plan," RFE/RL, November 20, 2007; Patrick Moore, "Russia, U.S. Conduct Joint Military Exercises [in Germany]," RFE/RL, December 14, 2007; Moore, "Russia, U.S. Plan Antiterrorism Exercises," RFE/RL, January 15, 2008.

10. C. J. Chivers, "Putin Proposes Alternatives for Missile Defense System," *New York Times,* June 9, 2007; Jim Rutenberg, "Putin Expands on His Missile Defense Plan," *New York Times,* July 3, 2007; Nazila Fatih, "Putin Is Said to Offer Idea on Standoff over Iran," *New York Times,* October 18, 2007; Patrick Moore, "Are Russia and U.S. Working toward 'Package Deal'?" RFE/RL, October 22, 2007; Brian Knowlton, "Gates Signals U.S. Could Delay E. Europe Missile Shield Plan," *Boston Globe,* October 24, 2007.

11. Jonas Bernstein, "[Russian President] Discusses Democracy with U.S. President over Dinner," RFE/RL, July 2, 2007; Thom Shanker, "Bush Sends Putin Missile Defense Offer," *New York Times,* March 18, 2008; Shanker, "Progress in U.S.-Russia Talks," *New York Times,* March 19, 2008.

12. Gregory Gleason, "The Uzbek Expulsion of U.S. Forces and Realignment in Central Asia," *Problems of Post-Communism* 53, 2 (March/April 2006): 49–60; Joshua Kucera, "Shanghai Cooperation Organization Summiteers Take Shots at U.S. Presence in Central Asia," Eurasia Insight, August 20, 2007, http://www.eurasianet.org; Kucera, "Uzbekistan: New U.S. Ambassador, New Policy?" Eurasia Insight, November 23, 2007, http://www.eurasianet.org; Richard Giragosian, "Uzbek President Meets Senior U.S. Military Commander," RFE/RL, January 25, 2008; "Stealth Move: American Troops to Return to Uzbekistan amid Thaw," Eurasia Insight, March 5, 2008, http://www.eurasianet.org. For a dissenting voice on the wisdom of such success, see Alexander Cooley, "U.S. Bases and Democratization in Central Asia," *Orbis* 52, 1 (Winter 2008): 65–90.

13. True, there is a range of projections, but they cluster around "more of the same for years on end": see Andrew C. Kuchins, "Alternative Futures for Russia to 2017," A Report of the Russia and Eurasia Program, Center for Strategic and International Studies (Washington, DC: CSIS Press, November 2007), http://www.csis.org.

14. A typical instance: as Armenia's 2008 crisis dragged on toward spring, its Foreign Ministry "expressed outrage over a statement made by U.S. Deputy Assistant Secretary Matthew Bryza, who characterized the actions of Armenian security forces on March 1 as 'harsh and brutal.' The Foreign Ministry on March 12 termed Bryza's comments 'groundless,' 'useless' and 'arbitrary.'" Yet the demonstrators probably wanted them to be stronger; see "Armenia: Officials, Opposition Take Tentative Steps toward Conciliation," Armenia: Vote 2008, March 12, 2008, http://www.eurasianet.org.

15. Leon Aron, "The United States and Russia: Ideologies, Policies, and Relations," *Russian Outlook* (Washington, DC: American Enterprise Institute for Public Policy Research, Summer 2006): 5, http://www.aei.org/docLib/20060629_20281ROSummer06_g.pdf.

Suggestions for
Further Reading

Introduction

McAuley, Mary. *Soviet Politics, 1917–1991.* Oxford: Oxford University Press, 1992.

Suny, Ronald Grigor. *The Revenge of the Past: Nationalism, Revolution, and the Collapse of the Soviet Union.* Stanford, CA: Stanford University Press, 1993.

I. The Weakness of Civil Society

Baker, Gideon. "The Taming of the Idea of Civil Society." In *Civil Society in Democratization,* edited by Peter Burnell and Peter Calvert, 43–71. London: Frank Cass, 2004.

Barber, Benjamin R. "Clansmen, Consumers, and Citizens: Three Takes on Civil Society." In *Civil Society, Democracy, and Civic Renewal,* edited by Robert K. Fullinwider, 9–29. Lanham, MD: Rowman & Littlefield, 1999.

Castoriadis, Cornelius. *The Imaginary Institution of Society.* Cambridge, MA: MIT Press, 1987.

Human Rights Watch. *Choking on Bureaucracy: State Curbs on Independent Civil Society Activism.* HRW Report Index no. D2001, February 20, 2008, http://hrw.org/reports/2008/russia0208/.

Cook, Linda J., and Elena Vinogradova. "NGOs and Social Policy-Making in Russia's Regions." *Problems of Post-Communism* 53, 5 (September–October 2006): 28–41.

Dahrendorf, Ralf. *Reflections on the Revolution in Europe.* New Brunswick, NJ: Transaction Publishers, 2005. First published 1990.

Evans, Jr., Alfred B., Laura A. Henry, and Lisa McIntosh Sundstrom, eds. *Russian Civil Society: A Critical Assessment.* Armonk, NY: M.E. Sharpe, 2006.

Migdal, Joel S. *Strong Societies and Weak States: State-Society Relations and State Capabilities in the Third World.* Princeton, NJ: Princeton University Press, 1988.

Trevisani, Tommaso. "After the Kolkhoz: Rural Elites in Competition." *Central Asian Survey* 26, 1 (March 2007): 85–104.

II. Politics as Elite Infighting

Beissinger, Mark R. "The Persistence of Empire in Eurasia." Presidential Address at 19th AAASS National Convention, November 19, 2007, *AAASS Newsnet* 48, 1 (January 2008): 1–8.

Brubaker, Rogers. *Nationalism Reframed: Nationhood and the National Question in the New Europe.* Cambridge: Cambridge University Press, 1996.

Bunce, Valerie, and Sharon Wolchik. "Democratizing Elections in the Postcommunist World: Definitions, Dynamics and Diffusion." *St. Antony's International Review* 2, 2 (Winter 2007): 64–79.

Bunce, Valerie, with Sharon Wolchik. "Favorable Conditions and Electoral Revolutions." *Journal of Democracy* 17 (October 2006): 7–18.

Fish, M. Steven. *Democracy Derailed in Russia: The Failure of Open Society.* Cambridge: Cambridge University Press, 2005.

Hale, Henry E. "Regime Cycles, Democracy, Autocracy, and Revolution in Post-Soviet Eurasia." *World Politics* 58 (October 2005): 133–165.

Kopstein, Jeffrey S., and David A. Reilly. "Geographic Diffusion and the Transformation of the Postcommunist World." *World Politics,* 53 (October 2000): 1–37.

III. The Politics of Economics and Sovereignty

Åslund, Anders. *Russia's Capitalist Revolution: Why Market Reform Succeeded and Democracy Failed.* Washington, DC: Peterson Institute of International Economics, 2007.

Jones-Luong, Pauline, and Erika Weinthal. "Prelude to the Resource Curse: Explaining Oil and Gas Development Strategies in the Soviet Successor States and Beyond." *Comparative Political Studies* 34, 4 (May 2001): 367–399.

Goldman, Marshall I. *Petrostate: Putin, Power, and the New Russia.* Oxford: Oxford University Press, 2008.

Tsygankov, Andrei P. "If Not Tanks, then by Banks? The Role of Soft Power in Putin's Foreign Policy." *Europe-Asia Studies* 58, 7 (November 2006): 1079–1099.

Tsygankov, Andrei P. *Pathways after Empire: National Identity and Foreign Economic Policy in the Post-Soviet World.* Lanham, MD: Rowman & Littlefield, 2003.

IV. States, Nations, and Nationalisms in Eurasia

Anderson, Benedict, *Imagined Communities: Reflections on the Origin and Spread of Nationalism.* London: Verso, 1983.

Barrington, Lowell W., ed. *After Independence: Making and Protecting the Nation in Postcolonial and Postcommunist States.* Ann Arbor: University of Michigan Press, 2006.

Doyle, Michael W. *Empires.* Ithaca, NY: Cornell University Press, 1986.

Gellner, Ernest. *Nations and Nationalism.* Ithaca, NY: Cornell University Press, 1983.

Hosking, Geoffrey A. *Rulers and Victims: The Russians in the Soviet Union.* Cambridge, MA: Harvard University Press, 2006.

———. *Russia and the Russians: A History.* Cambridge, MA: Harvard University Press, 2001.

Lapidus, Gail W. "Ethnicity and State-Building: Accommodating Ethnic Differences in Post-Soviet Eurasia." In *Beyond State Crisis? Postcolonial Africa and Post-Soviet Eurasia in Comparative Perspective,* edited by Mark R. Beissinger and Crawford Young, 323–358. Baltimore: Johns Hopkins University Press, 2002.

McFaul, Michael. "The Fourth Wave of Democracy *and* Dictatorship:

Noncooperative Transitions in the Postcommunist World." *World Politics* 54 (January 2002): 212–244.

Shulman, Stephen. "National Identity and Public Support for Political and Economic Reform in Ukraine." *Slavic Review* 64, 1 (Spring 2005): 59–83.

Snyder, Jack L. *Myths of Empire: Domestic Politics and International Ambition.* Ithaca, NY: Cornell University Press, 1991.

V. Today's Eurasia and the United States

Baev, Pavel K. "Chimera of a 'New Cold War' in the Russia-U.S. Relations [*sic*]." *AAASS Newsnet* 47, 5 (October 2007): 1–8.

Kuchins, Andrew C. "Alternative Futures for Russia to 2017." A Report of the Russia and Eurasia Program, Center for Strategic and International Studies. Washington, DC: CSIS Press, November 2007. http://www.csis.org.

INDEX

Abdelal, Rawi, 65
Abramovich, Roman, 64, 74
Akayev, Askar, 41, 61
Albright, Madeleine, 89
"Alternative Futures" (Center for
    Strategic and International
    Studies, 2007), 130, 165n13
Armenia, 2, 61–62, 165n14
    ethnic nationalism, 97
Aron, Leon, 138–139
assistance
    See Western aid
authoritarianism
    determinants of, 50–51
    See also competitive authoritari-
        anism; presidentialism;
        strongman rule
Azerbaijan
    ethnic nationalism, 97
    natural resources, 6, 68
    oil and gas revenues, 76–77

Bakiyev, Kurmanbek, 104
Balmaceda, Margarita M., 163n38

Baltic republics, 2, 45
    See also Estonia; Latvia;
        Lithuania
Balzer, Harley, 78–79
Beissinger, Mark P., 163n37
Belarus
    governance of, 59–60
    language laws, 104
    Russia and, 115, 163n38
Berdymukhammedov,
    Gurbanguly, 35, 52
Berezovsky, Boris, 74
Borat (film), 112
Brezhnev, Leonid, 50
Broers, Lawrence, 148n22
Bryza, Matthew, 165n14
Burke, Edmund, 122
Bush, George W., 13, 72–73, 74,
    125

Caspian Basin pipeline diplomacy,
    68, 72, 85–86
Central Asian Cooperation Orga-
    nization (CACO), 48

Envoi

If you at last must have a word to say,
Say neither, in their way,
"It is deadly magic and accursed,"
Nor "It is blest," but only "It is here."

Stephen Vincent Benet, *John Brown's Body*